Kingston Ontario Book 5 in Colour Photos, Saving Our History One Photo at a Time

Photography
by Barbara Raué
2016

Series Name:
Cruising Ontario

Book 144: Kingston Book 5

Cover photo: 96 Albert Street, Page 6

Series Name: Cruising Ontario
Saving Our History One Photo at a Time in colour photos

Books Available in Alphabetical Order:
Aberfoyle, Acton, Alton, Ancaster, Arthur, Aylmer, Ayr, Bloomingdale, Brantford, Burlington, Caledon, Caledonia, Cambridge, Clifford, Conestogo, Delhi, Dorchester to Aylmer, Drayton, Drumbo, Dundas, Eden Mills, Elmira, Elora, Fergus, Guelph, Hagersville, Hamilton, Hanover, Harriston, Hespeler, Jarvis, Kitchener, Linwood, Listowel, London, Lucknow, Mono, Mount Forest, Neustadt, New Hamburg, Niagara-on-the-Lake, Oakville, Orangeville, Orillia, Owen Sound, Palmerston, Peterborough, Port Elgin, Preston, Rockwood, Seaforth, Sheffield, Shelburne, Simcoe, Southampton, St. Jacobs, St. Thomas, Stoney Creek, Stratford, Tillsonburg, Waterdown, Waterford, Waterloo, Wellesley, Wingham

Book 114-116: Waterloo
Book 117-119: Windsor
Book 120-121: Amherstburg
Book 122: Essex
Book 123-124: Kingsville
Book 125-127: Woodstock
Book 128: Thamesford
Book 129: St. Mary's
Book 133-136: Sarnia
Book 137: Petrolia
Book 138-139: Welland
Book 140-145: Kingston

Other Books by Barbara Raue

Coins of Gold

Arrows, Indians and Love

The Life and Times of Barbara
Volume 1: Inventions That Have Enhanced My Life
Volume 2: Entertainment That I Have Enjoyed
Volume 3: East Coast Trips
Volume 4: Olympics Have Always Intrigued Me
Volume 5: Wonders of the World
Volume 6: Caribbean Cruises We Have Enjoyed
Volume 7: Animals
Volume 8: Storms and Other Major Disasters in My Lifetime
Volume 9: Wars, Terrorist Attacks and Major Disasters

The Cromwell Family Book

Laura Secord Discovered

Daddy Where Are You?

Visit Barbara's website to view all of her books
http://barbararaue.ca

Table of Contents

Kingston is a historic city an equal-distance from Toronto, Montreal and Ottawa, where the St. Lawrence River meets Lake Ontario and the Rideau Canal.

In October 1783, Captain William Redford Carleton of the King's Royal Regiment of New York, met with the local Mississauga Indians. Crawford, acting for the British government, purchased from the Mississaugas a large tract of land east of the Bay of Quinte. In September 1783, Deputy Surveyor-General John Collins laid out townships for settlers. Loyalists who wanted to continue living under British rule came to Kingston after the American Revolution; many had been forced to leave their homes in the new United States.

Molly Brant (Degonwadonti) was born about 1736 into a prominent Mohawk family. About 1759 she became the wife of William Johnson, Superintendent of Indian Affairs for Britain's Northern Colonies, and was a powerful figure there. Well-educated and a powerful speaker, Molly Brant wielded great influence among the Iroquois and was responsible for much of Johnson's success in dealing with them. Following the outbreak of the American Revolution she and her younger brother Joseph played a leading role in persuading the Confederacy to support Britain. In 1777, she fled to Canada and after the war, in recognition of her services, she was granted a pension by the government. She settled in Cataraqui (Kingston) where she died in 1796. She is buried in the Anglican Church Lower Burial Ground.

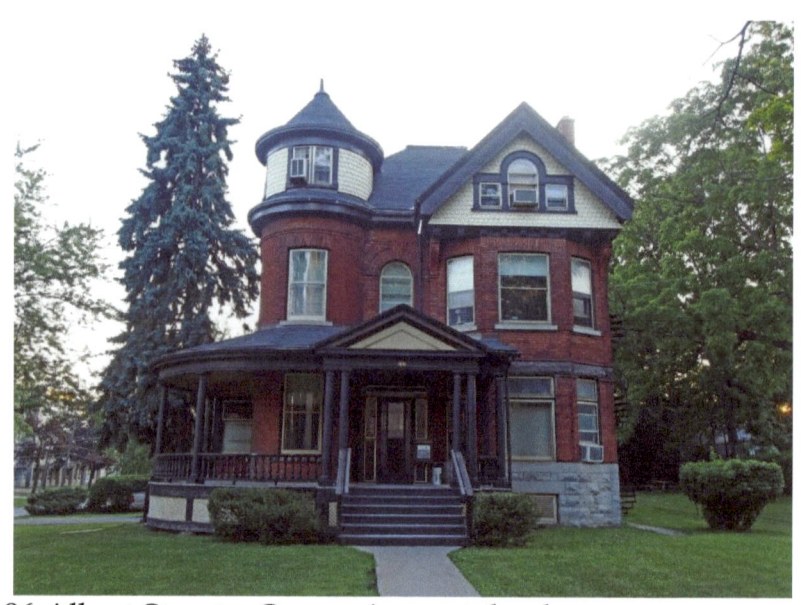

96 Albert Street – Queen Anne style, three-storey turret, Palladian window above two-storey bay window, pediment, voussoirs with keystone

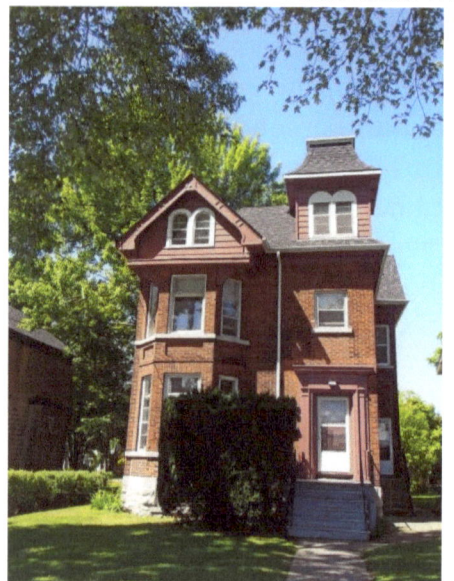

152 Albert Street
3 storey tower, 2 storey bay

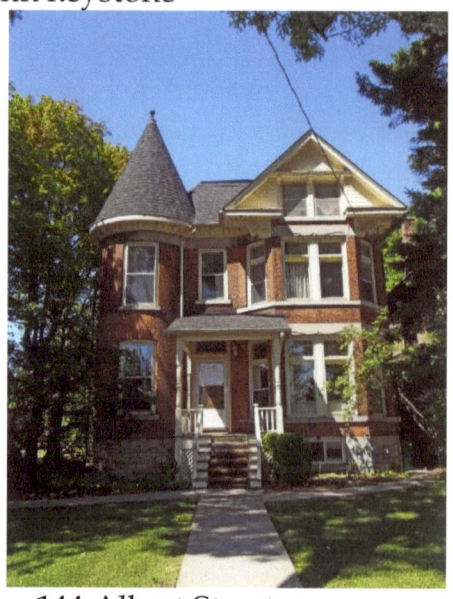

144 Albert Street
2 storey turret, 2 storey bay

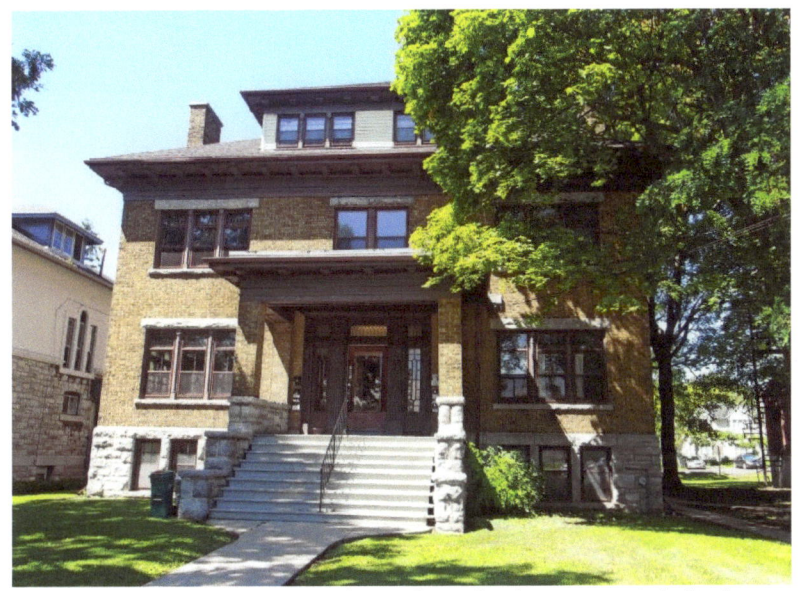

142 Albert Street – hipped roof with dormer, sidelights and transom

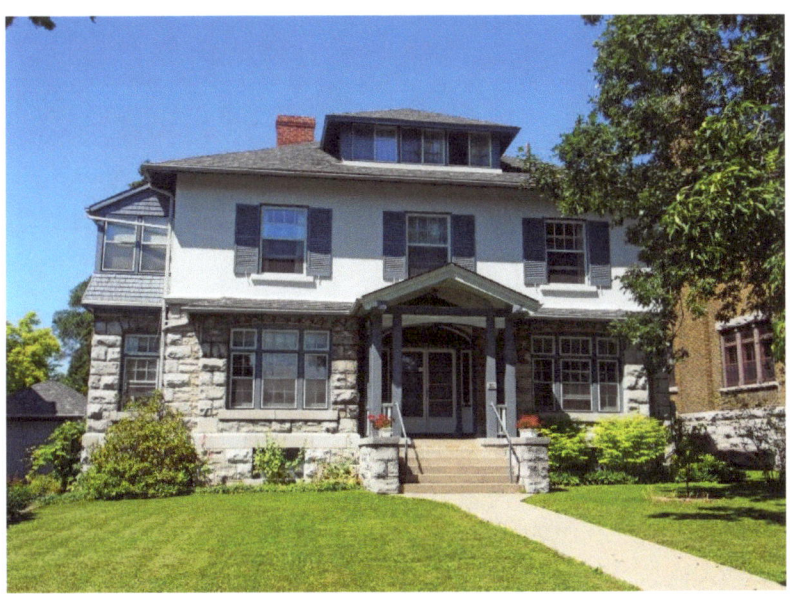

138 Albert Street – Italianate, stone, hipped roof with shed dormer, pediment above door, sidelights and transom

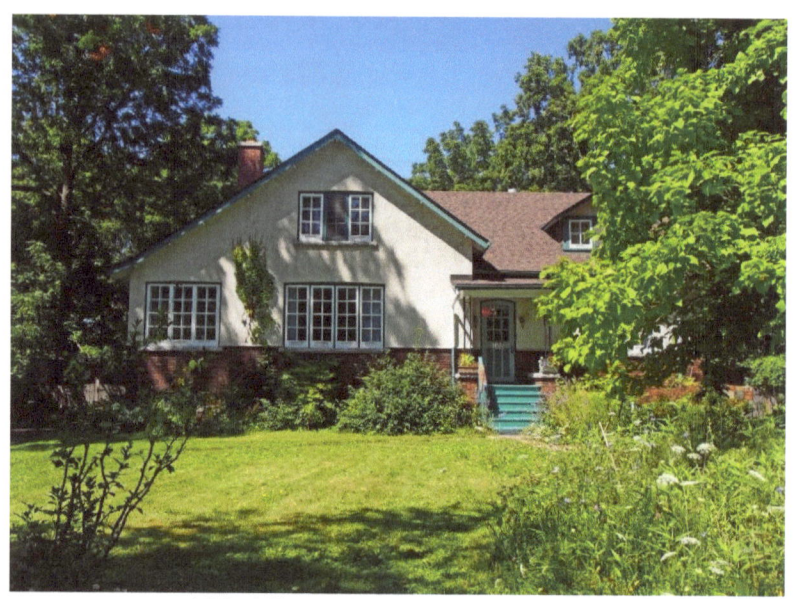

108 Albert Street - vernacular

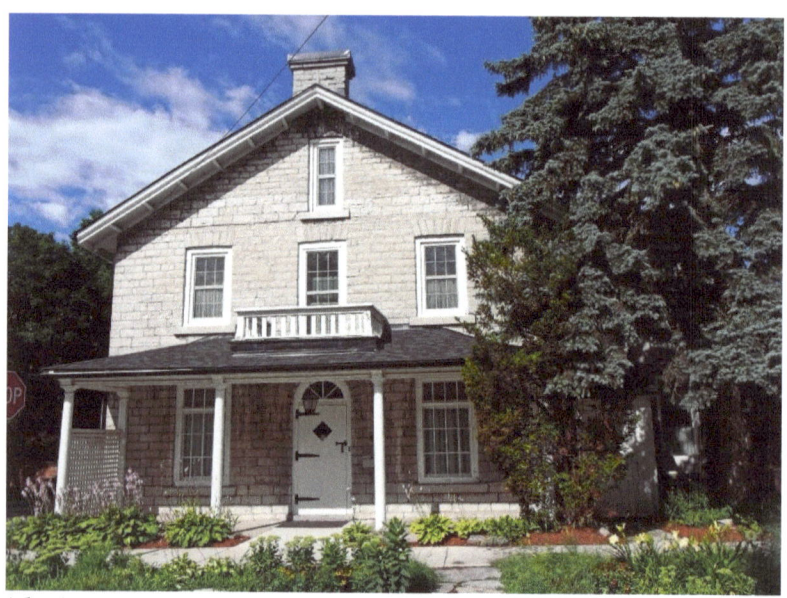

2 Alwington Avenue – c. 1850 – stone, Gothic, second floor balcony, transom window - A very well kept up nineteenth century home.

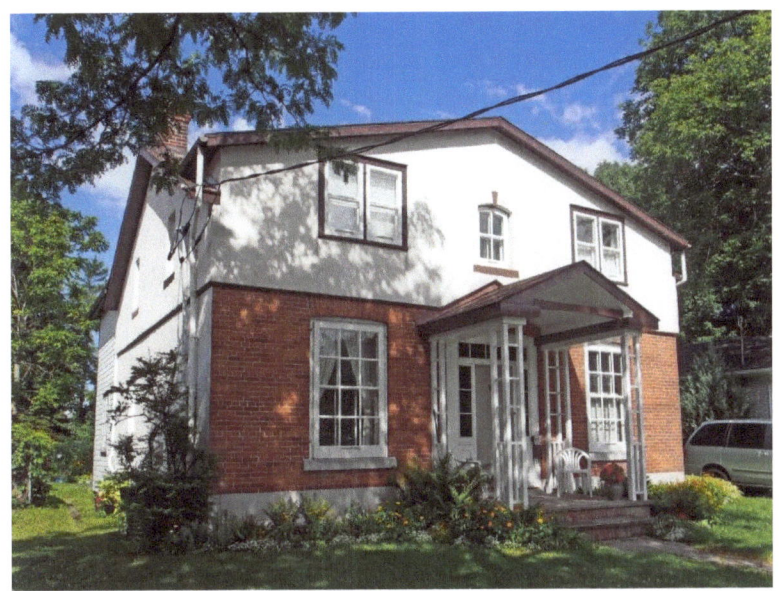

18 Alwington Ave – Vernacular – pediment, keystone, sidelights and transom

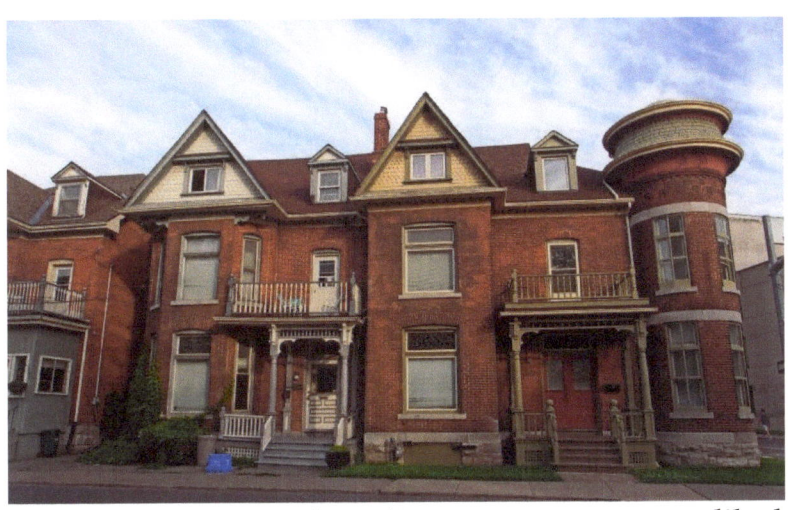

208-210 Bagot Street – Edwardian, two-storey tower-like bay, dormers

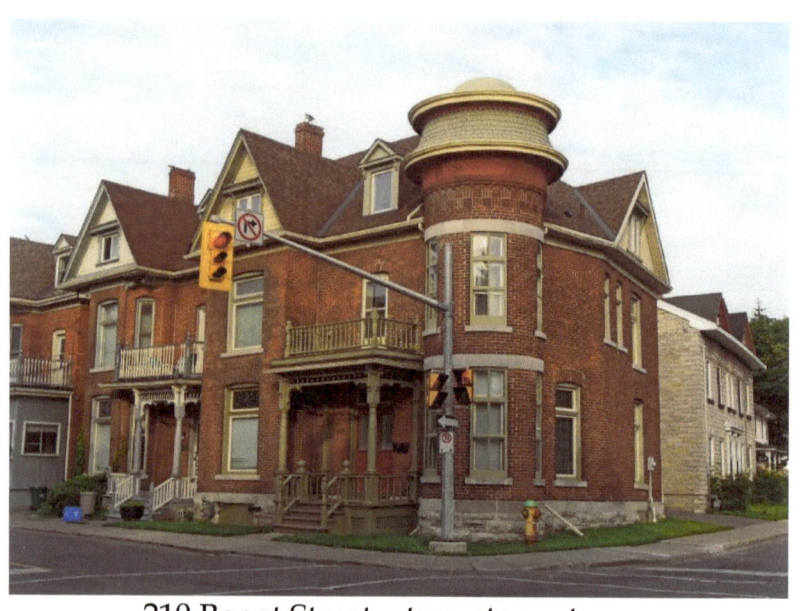

210 Bagot Street – two-storey tower

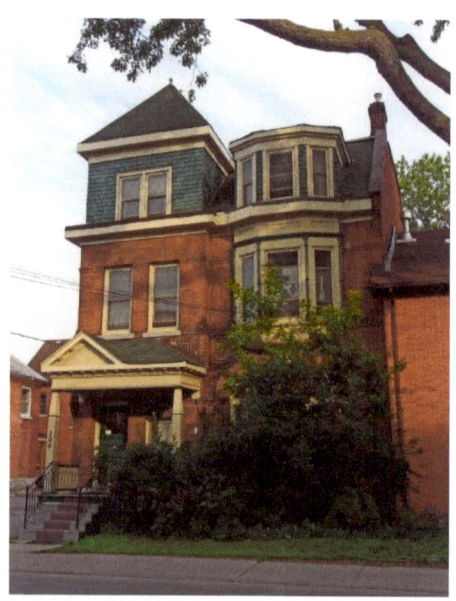

194 Bagot Street – three-storey tower-like frontispiece, pediment; three-storey tower-like bay

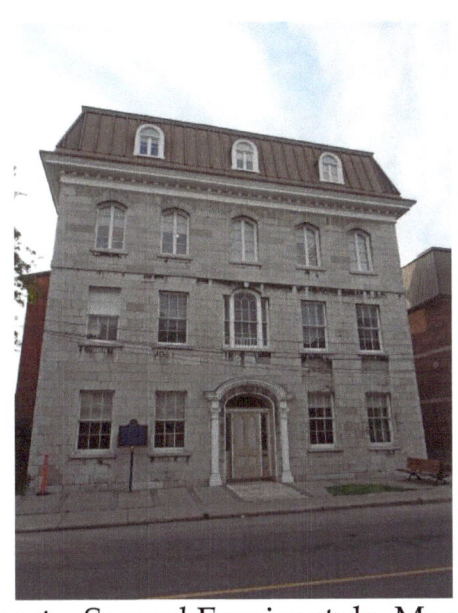

Bagot Street – Second Empire style, Mansard roof

Bishop Alexander MacDonell (1762-1840), patriot, colonizer and priest, was born in the highlands of Scotland. In 1804 he came to Canada as the chaplain of the disbanded Glengarry Fencibles and later became Auxiliary Bishop of Quebec. As the first Bishop of the Diocese of Kingston, formed in 1826, he lived in this building and in 1831 was appointed to the Legislative Council of Upper Canada. In 1837 he founded Regiopolis College in Kingston.

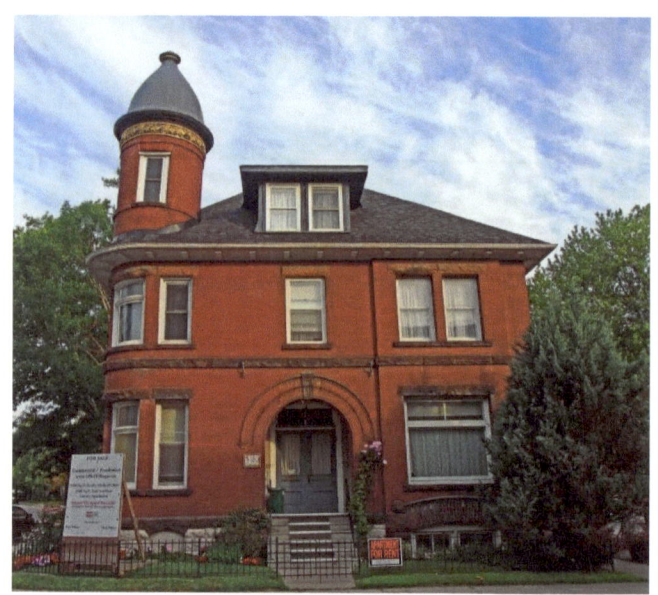

180 Bagot Street – 3-storey turret, hipped roof with dormer, banding, keystone above door

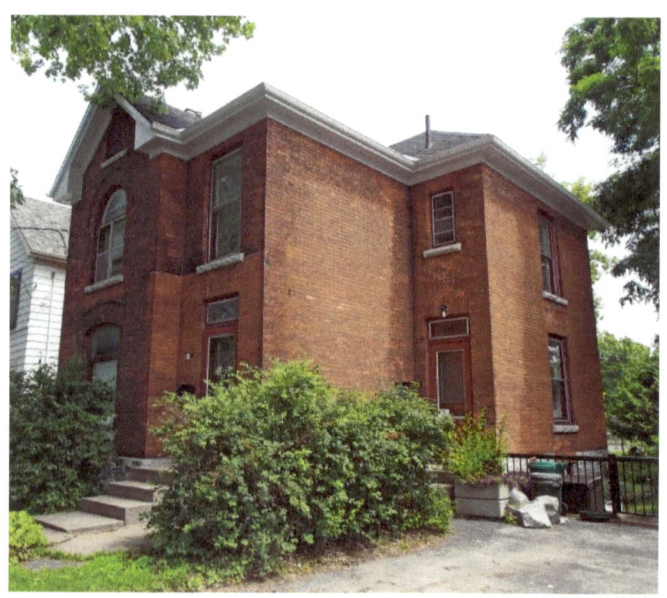

170 Bagot Street – 2½ storey frontispiece

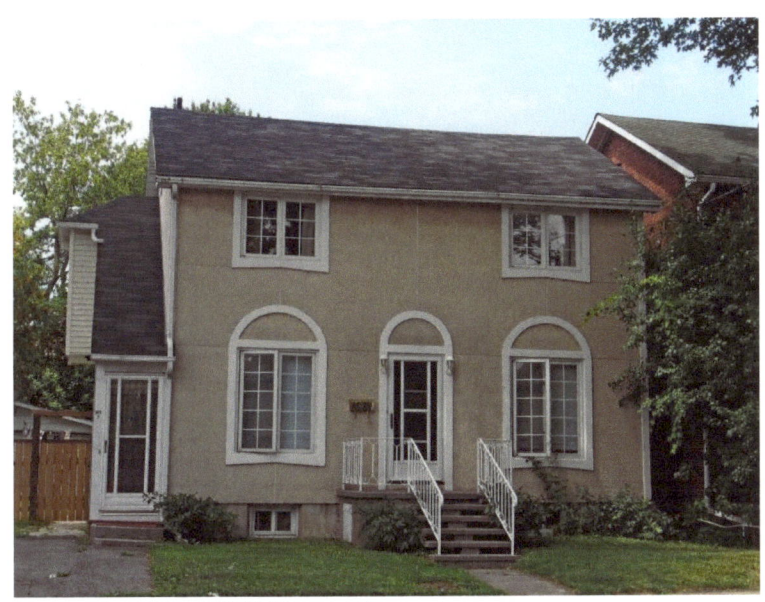

478 Bagot Street - stucco

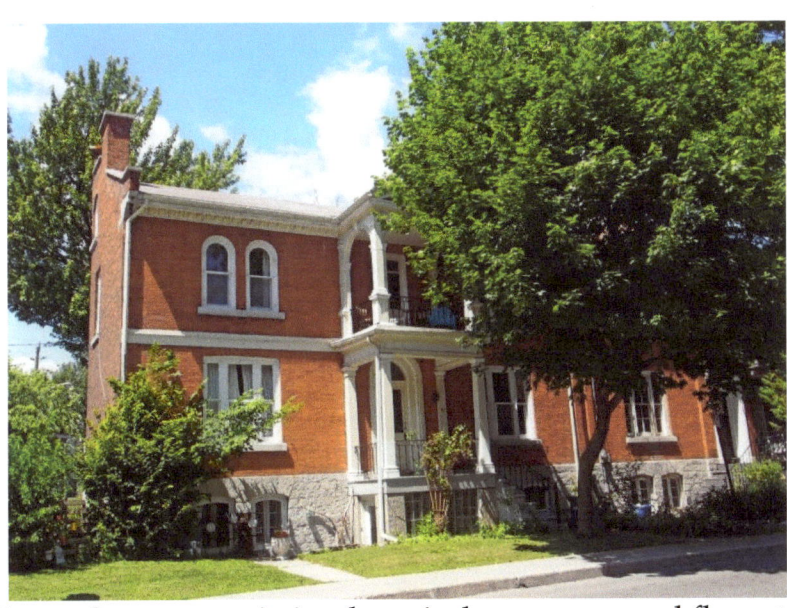

90 Bagot Street – semi-circular windows on second floor, two-storey columned porch topped with pediment

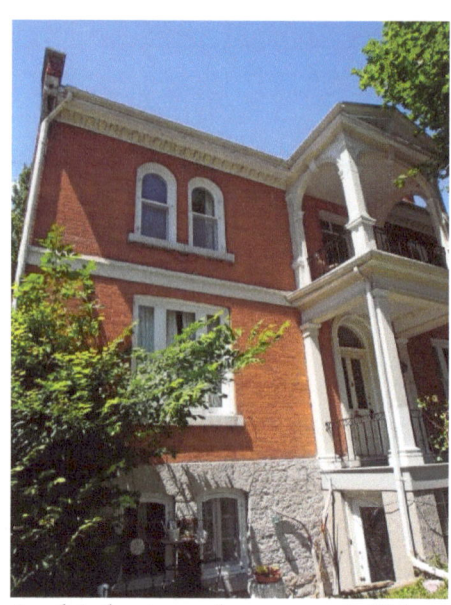

90 Bagot Street – high stone basement, 2½ storey red brick above

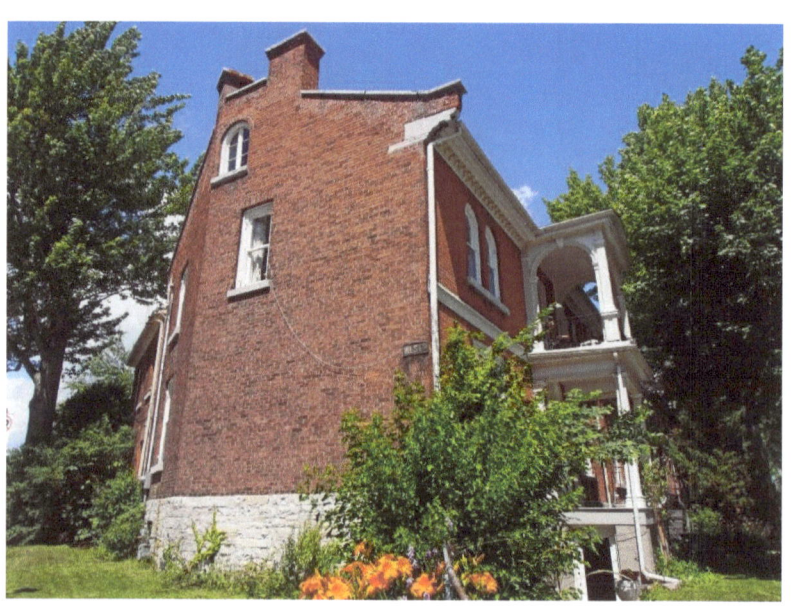

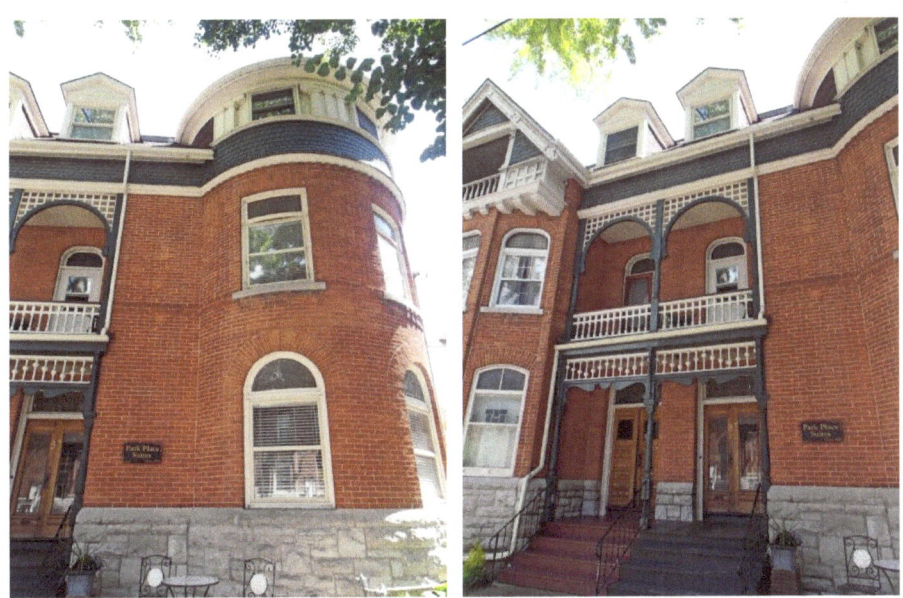

97-99 Bagot Street – three-storey circular tower, dormers, second floor verandah

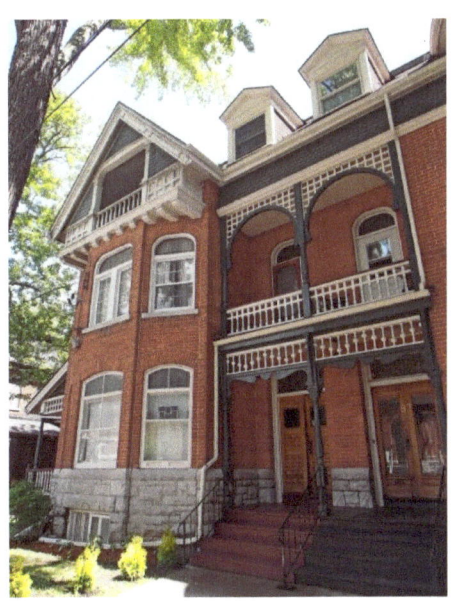

97-99 Bagot Street – Park Place Suites – c. 1860 – 2½ storey frontispiece with third floor sleeping porch; dormers in attic

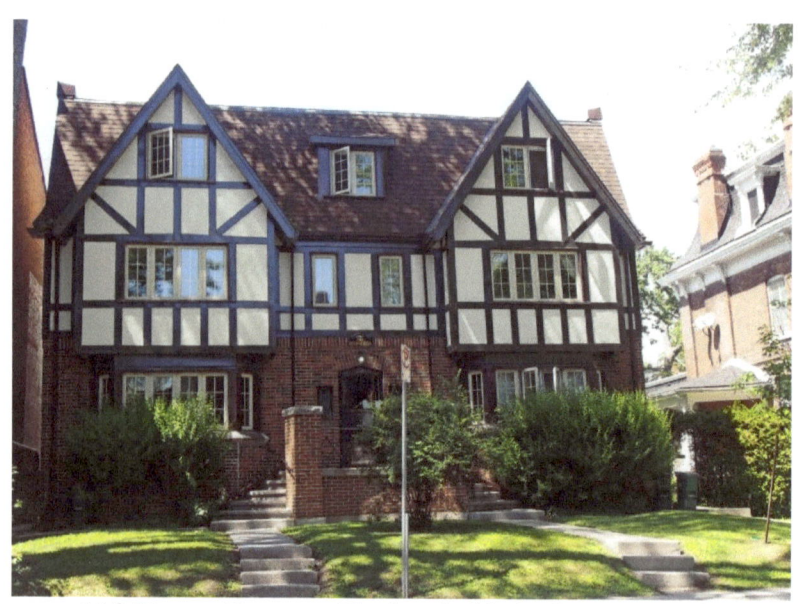

110 Bagot Street – Tudor half-timbering style

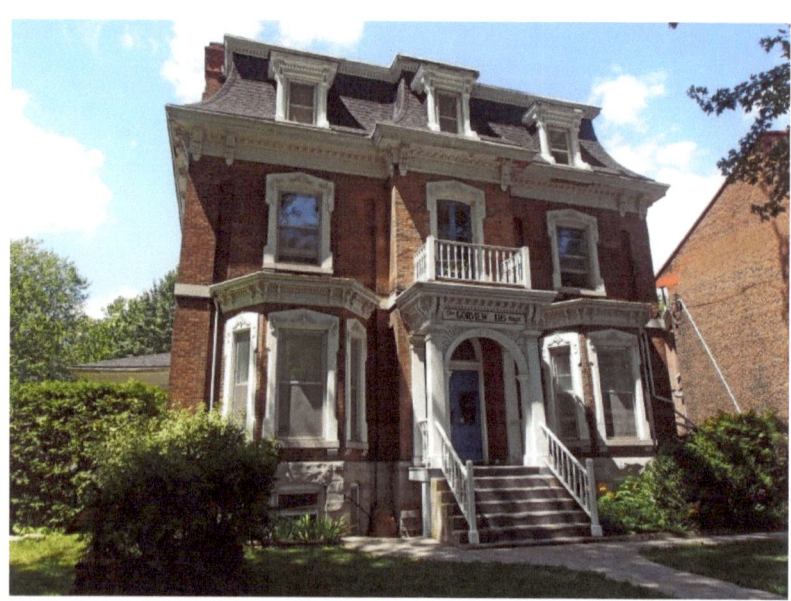

116 Bagot Street – Second Empire, Mansard roof with dormers and window hoods, second floor balcony, bay windows, cornice brackets, dentil moulding, pillared entrance

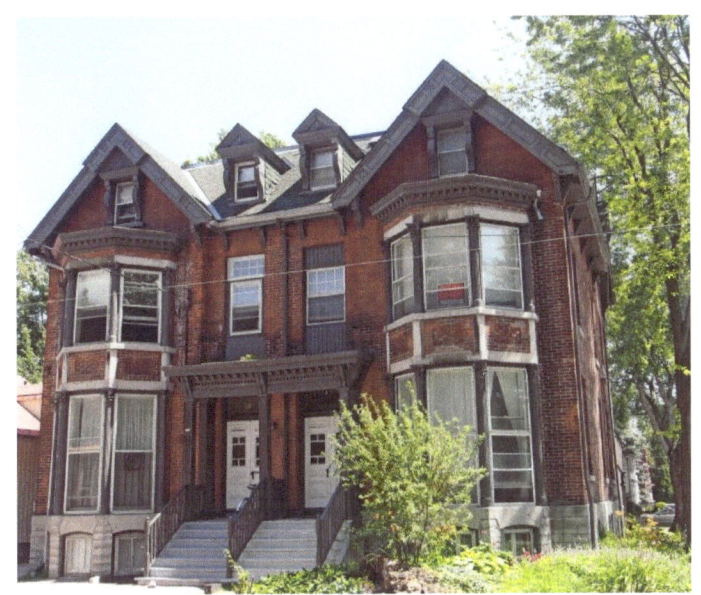

117-119 Bagot Street – two storey bay windows, dormers between gables

Beverley Street

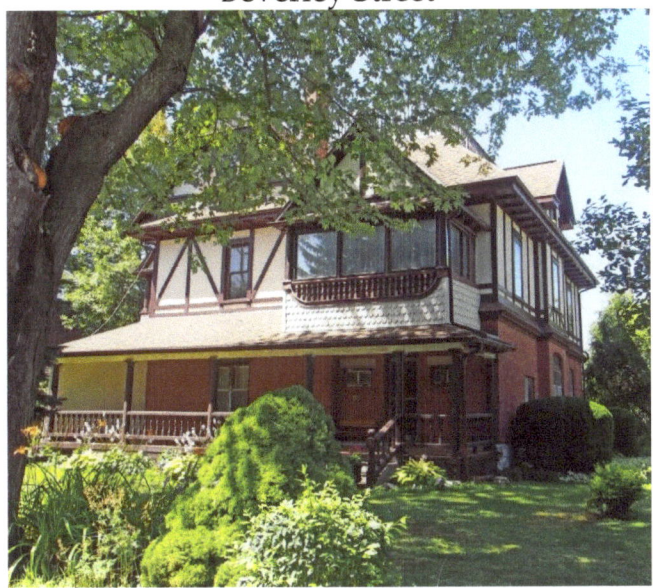

Tudor accents

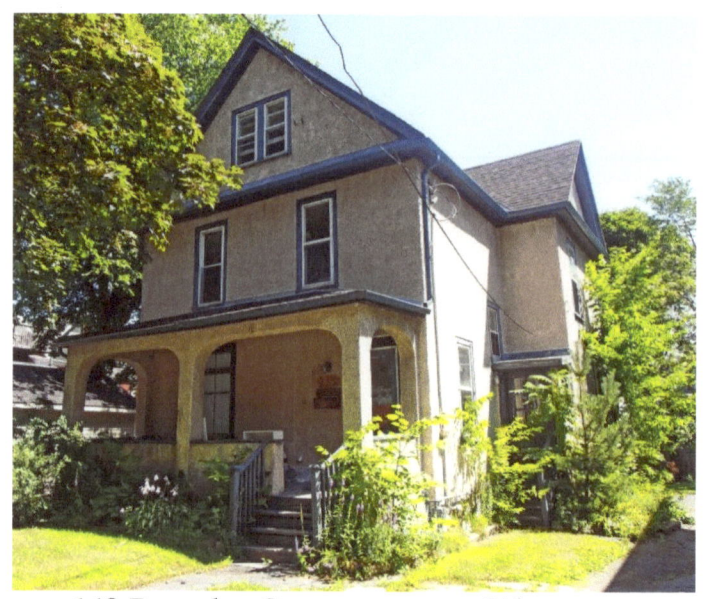

143 Beverley Street – stucco, 2½ storeys

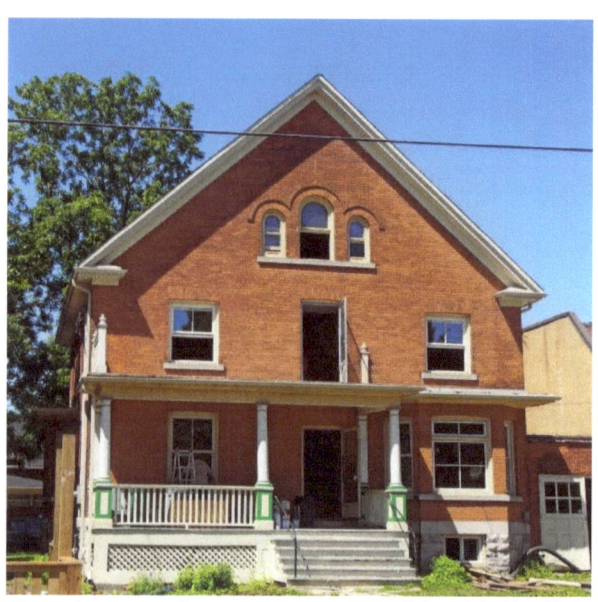

Beverley Street – cornice return on gable, Palladian window

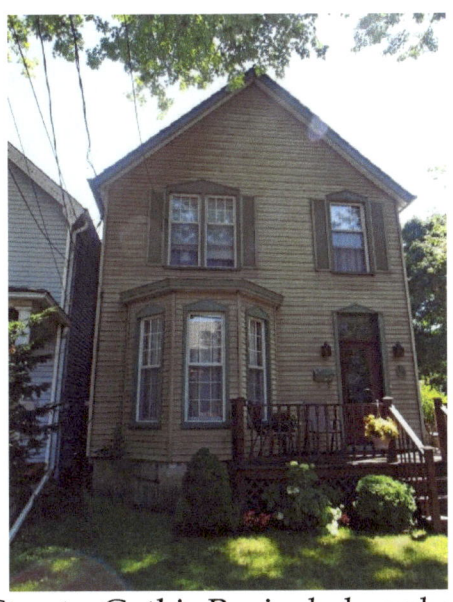

119 Beverley Street – Gothic Revival - board and batten, bay window, six-over-six sash windows

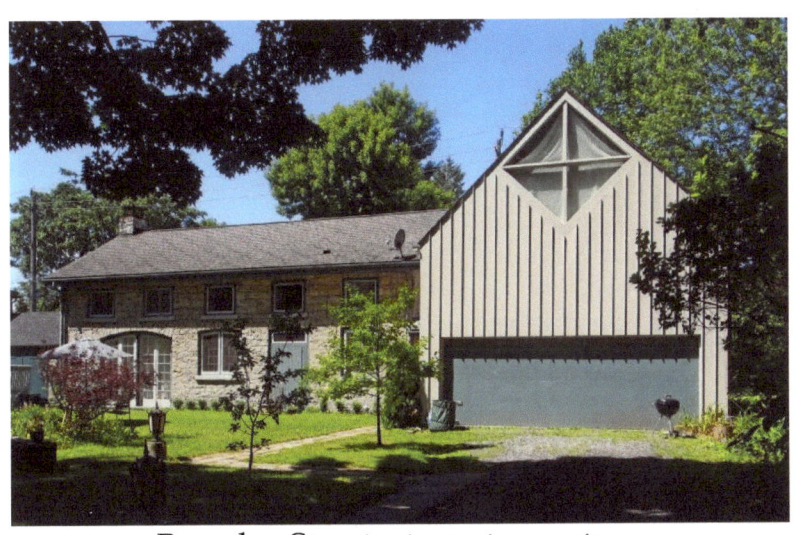

Beverley Street – two-storey stone

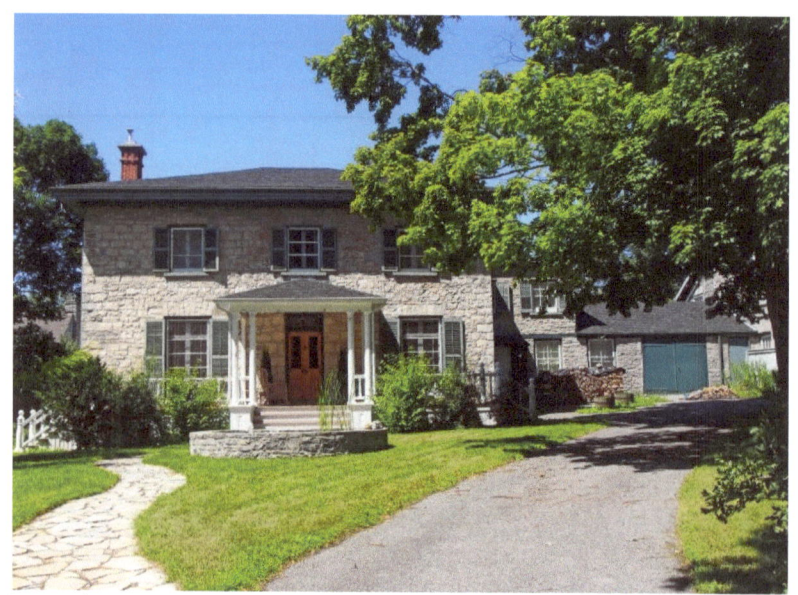

Beverley Street – two-storey stone building, hipped roof

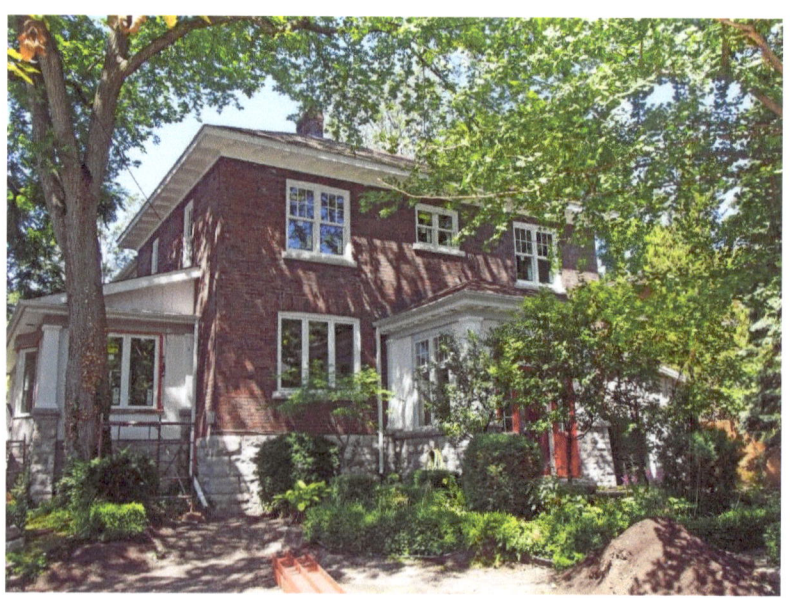

82 Beverley Street – red brick

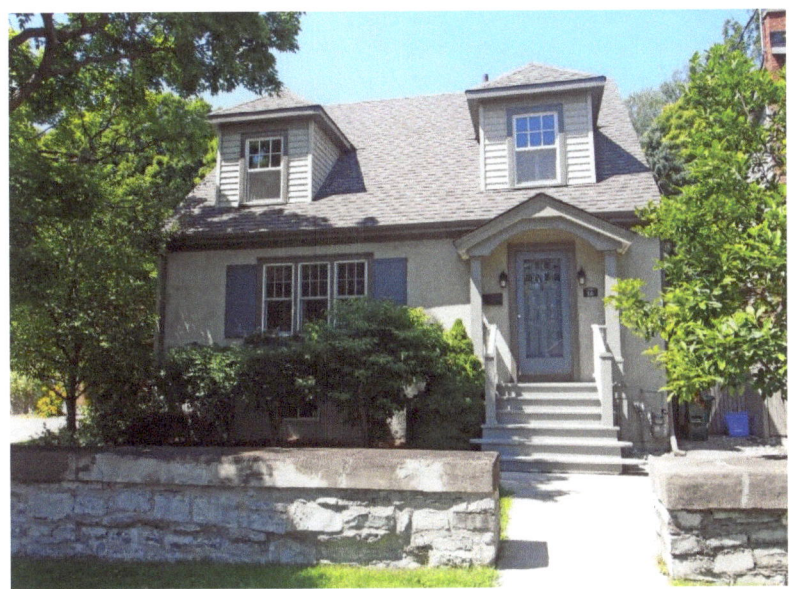

16 Beverley Street - dormers

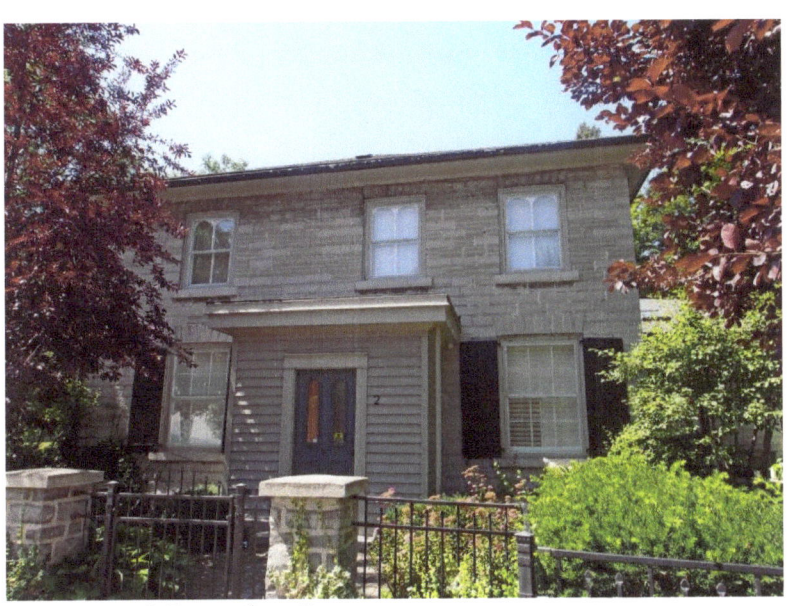

2 Beverley Street – two storey stone

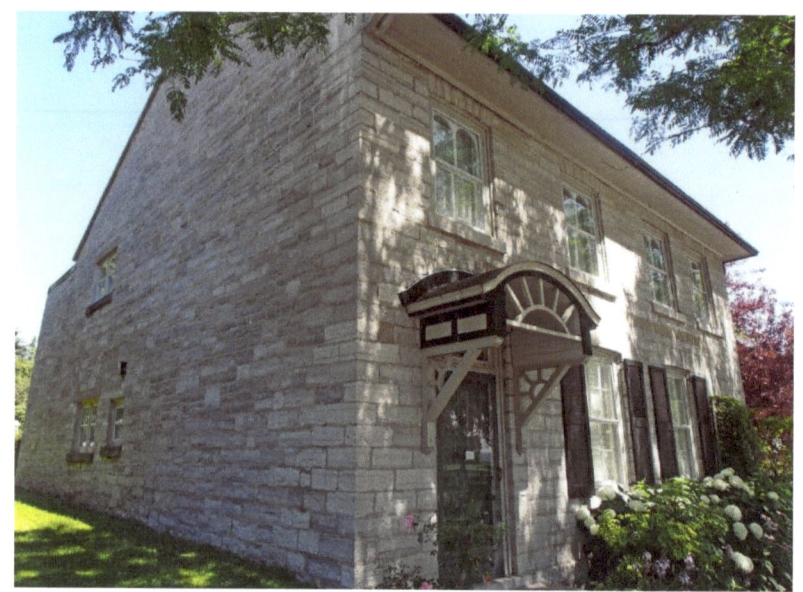

Beverley Street – stone

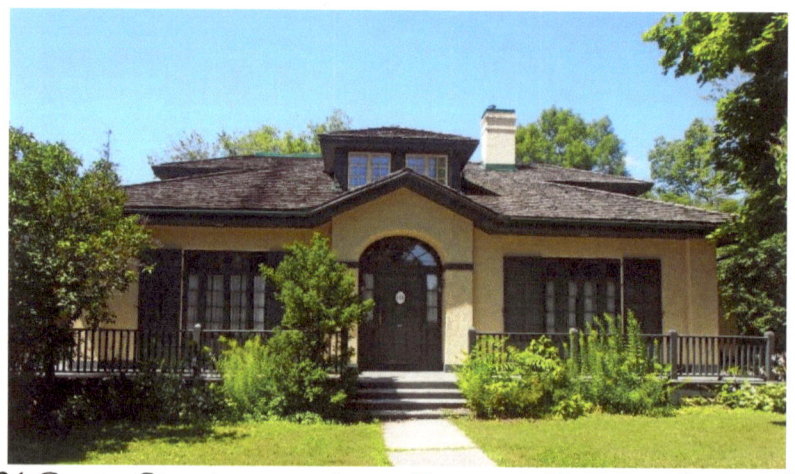

124 Centre Street – one-storey Regency Cottage, dormer in attic

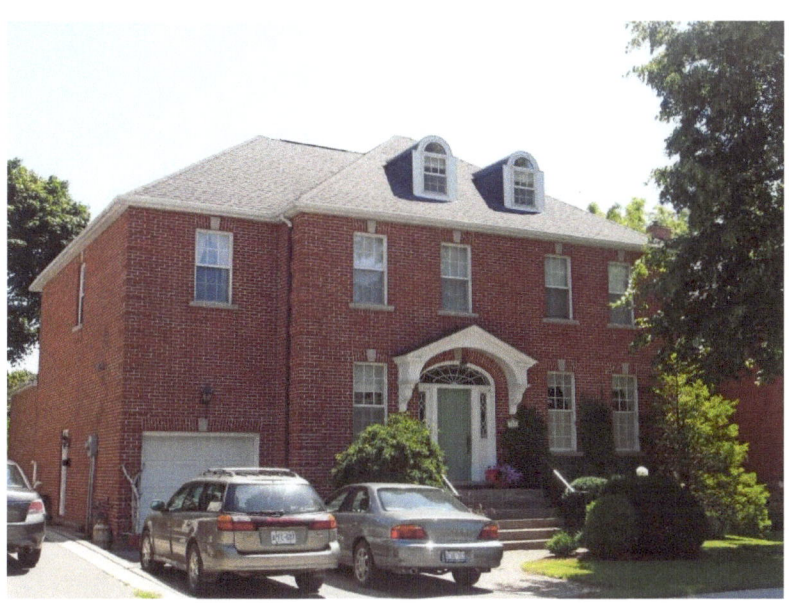

123 Centre Street – two storey red brick, dormers, corner quoins, voussoirs with keystones, engaged columns at entrance, sidelights and transom

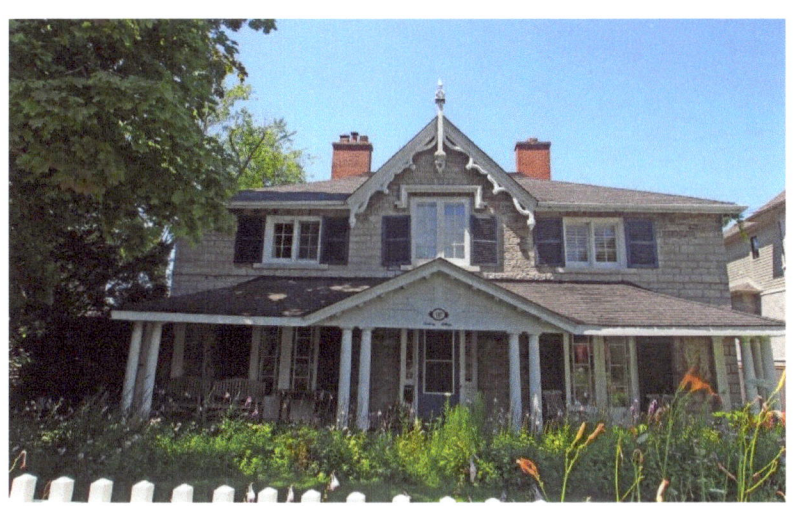

102 Centre Street – Barberry Cottage – Gothic – stone, gingerbread trim and finial on gable

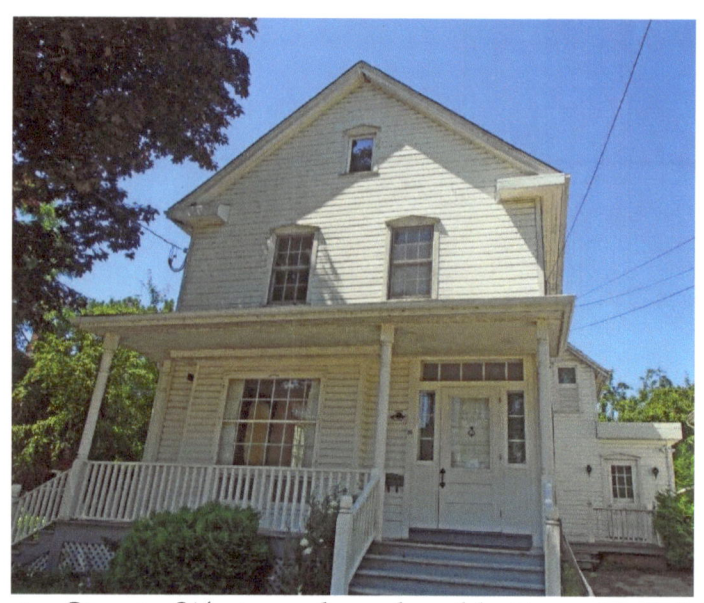

76 Centre Street - 2½ storey board and batten, sidelights and transom windows

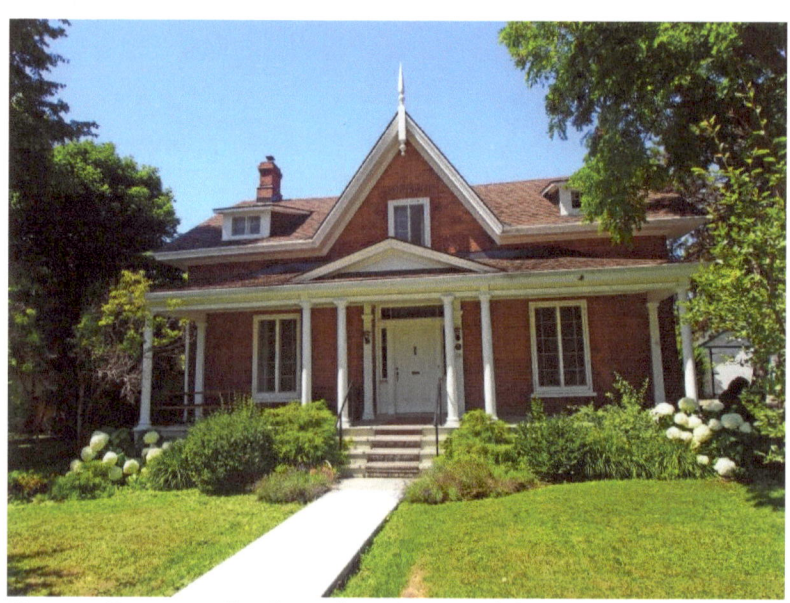

68 Centre Street – Gothic, finial on gable, dormers, sidelights and transom windows

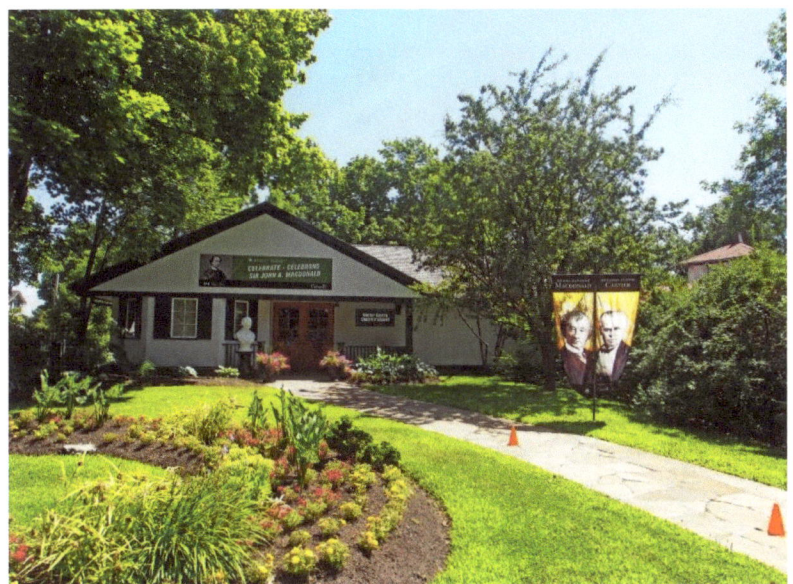

Sir John A. MacDonald Visitor Centre

Confederation (1867) was when Sir John A. MacDonald brought together four provinces (Ontario, Quebec, Nova Scotia and New Brunswick) and called it Canada. He was instrumental in the building of the Canadian Pacific Railway which helped people get from one part of Canada to another. The tracks were 4,660 kilometres long. He created the North West Mounted Police (1873-1904), the first police force in Canada.

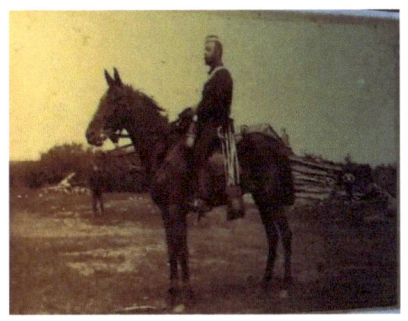

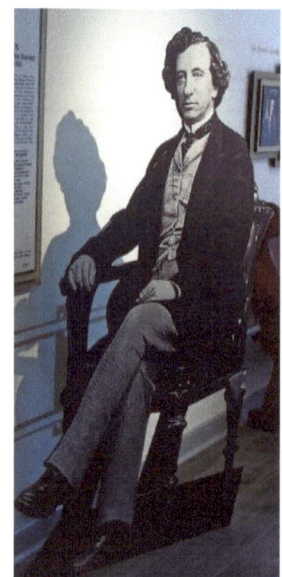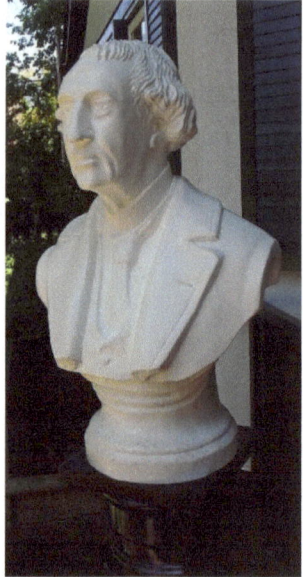

Sir John A. MacDonald

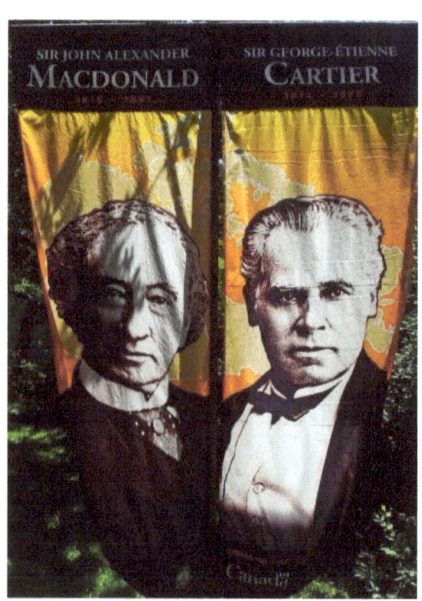

Sir John A. MacDonald and Sir George Etienne Cartier

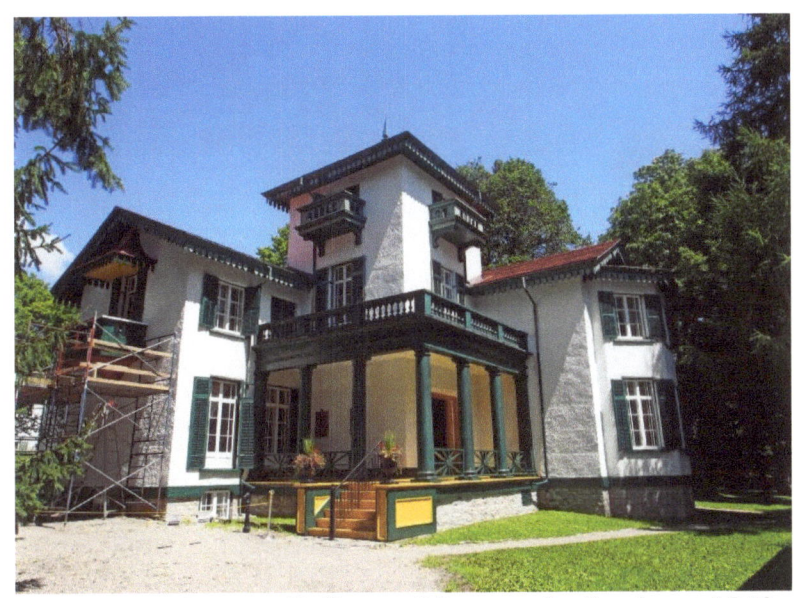

35 Centre Street - Bellevue House – built about 1840
– Italian Villa architecture

The central tower has an ornate cornice and a veranda with Doric columns and an architrave on the main floor and a balustraded terrace on the second floor. The windows have large shutters. The main floor has multipaned French Doors.

Bellevue House is a national historic site because of its association with Sir John A. MacDonald, a Father of Confederation and Canada's first prime minister, and because it is an outstanding example of Italianate architecture in the Picturesque manner.

John A. MacDonald lived here with his family from August 1848 to September 1849. At the time MacDonald was a lawyer and a Member for Kingston in the Legislative Assembly of the Province of Canada.

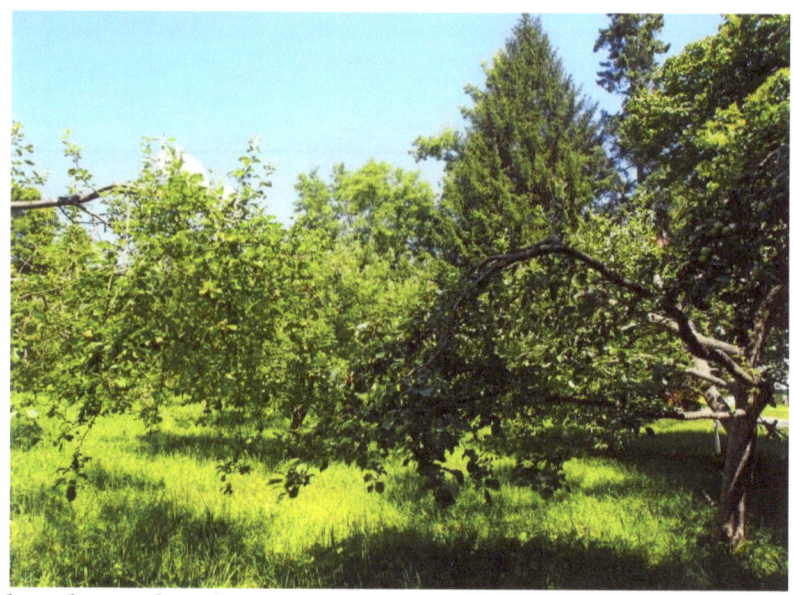

Today the orchard contains a collection of antique varieties of apple trees.

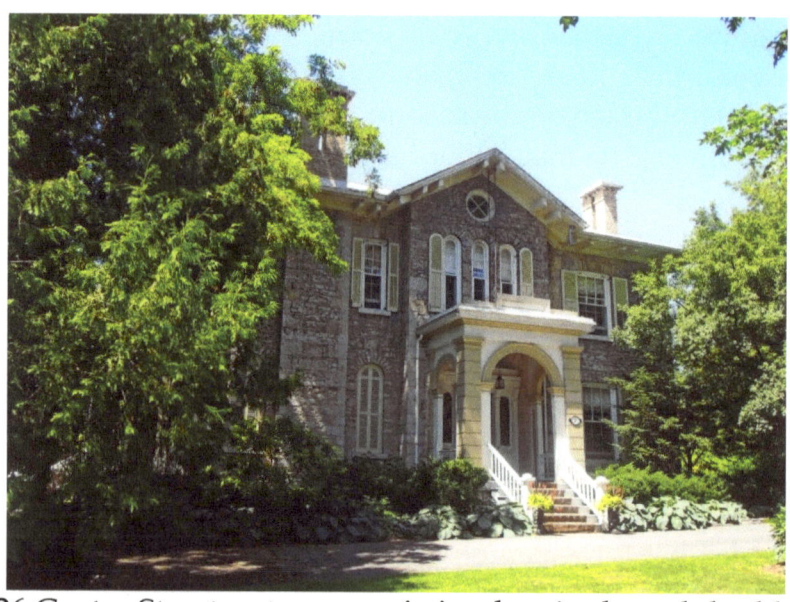

26 Centre Street – stone, semi-circular single and double windows, pillared entrance, tall chimneys

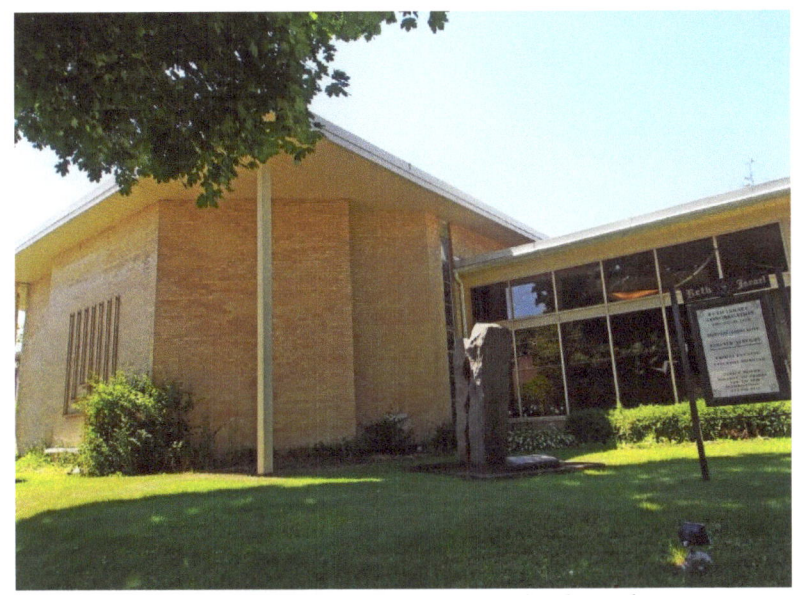

Centre Street – Beth Israel Church

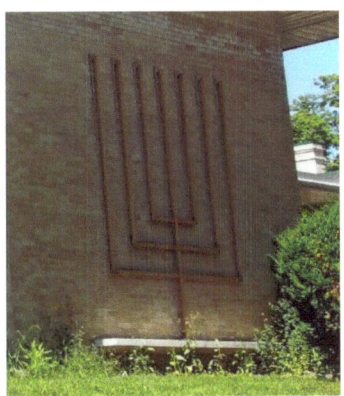

Menorah

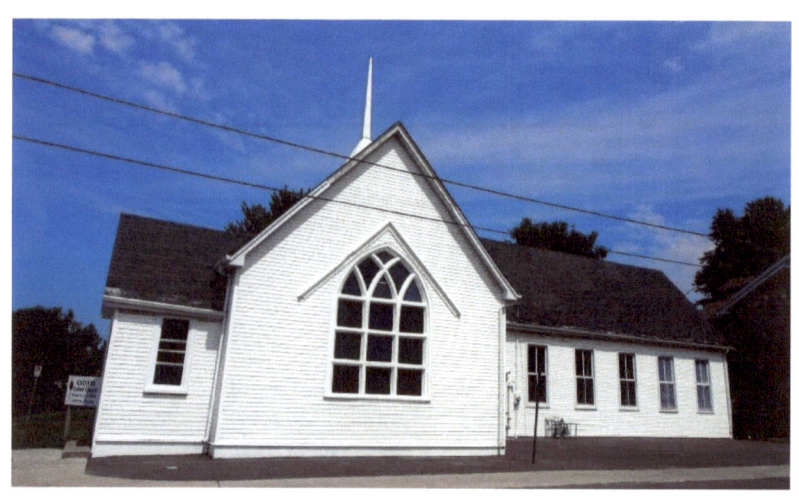

Charles Street – Calvary United Church

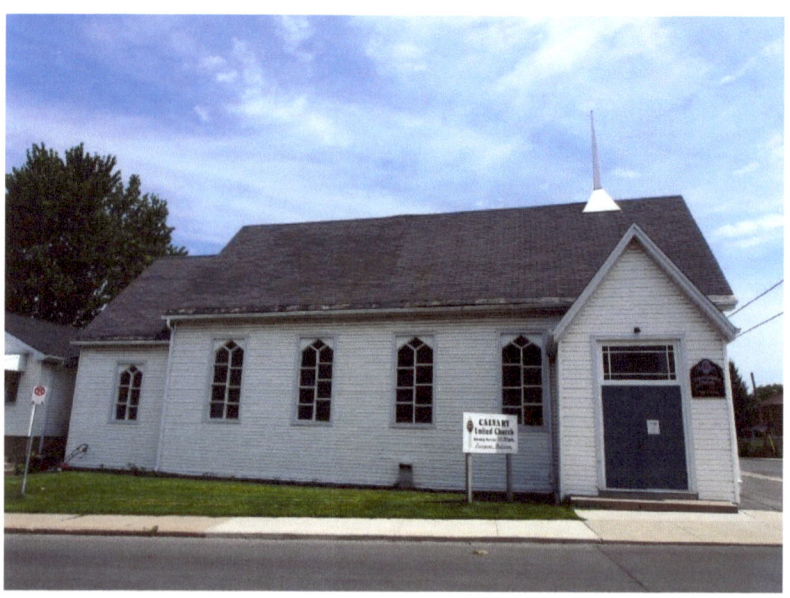

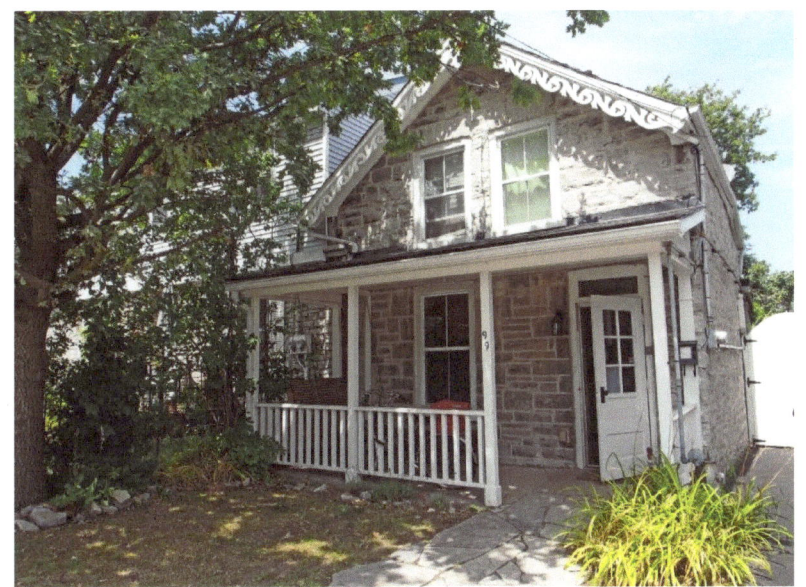

99 Charles Street

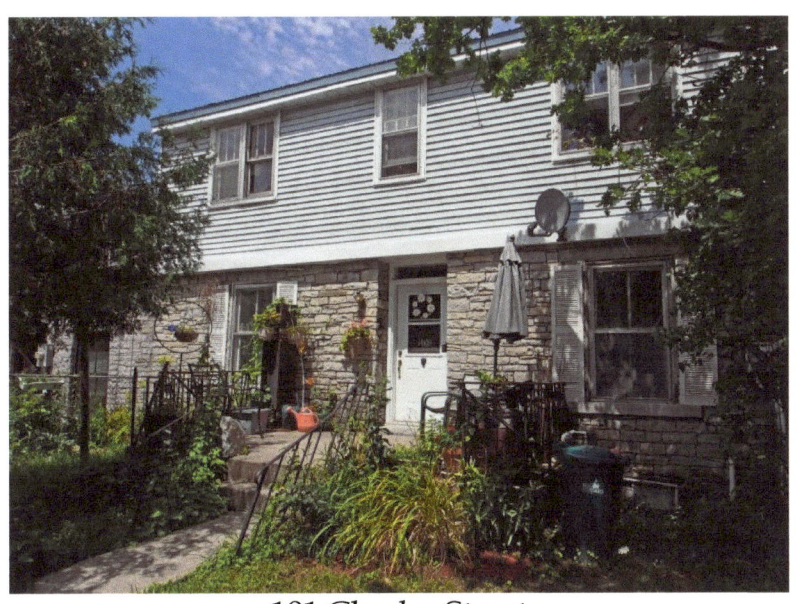

101 Charles Street

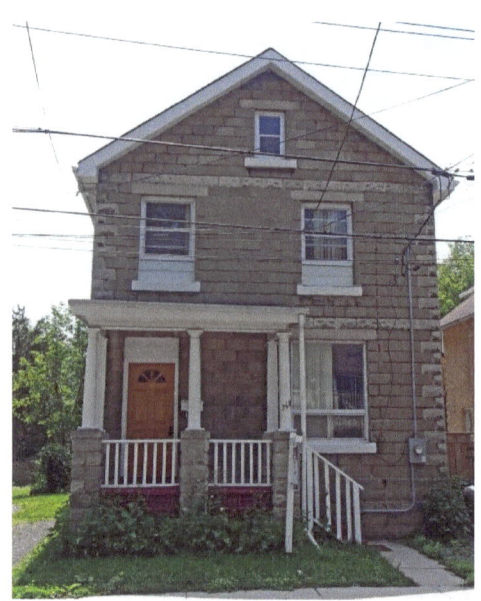

148 Charles Street

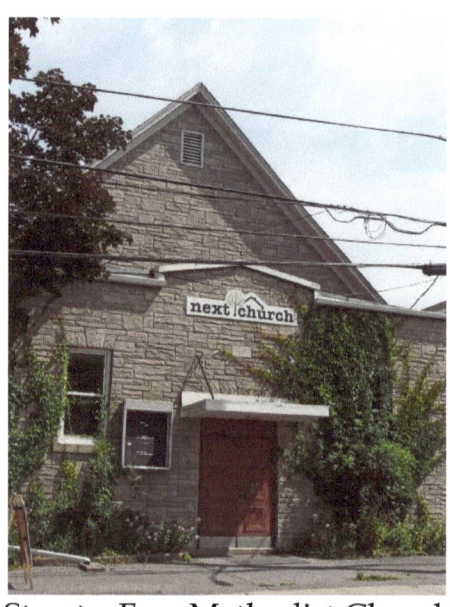

89 Colborne Street – Free Methodist Church – built 1907, rebuilt 1949

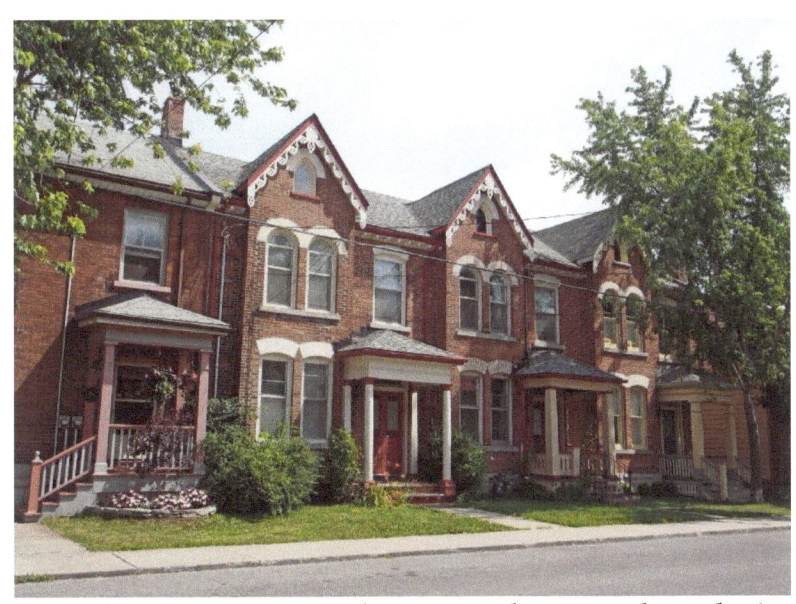

69-75 Colborne Street – Gothic Revival – verge board trim on gables, voussoirs

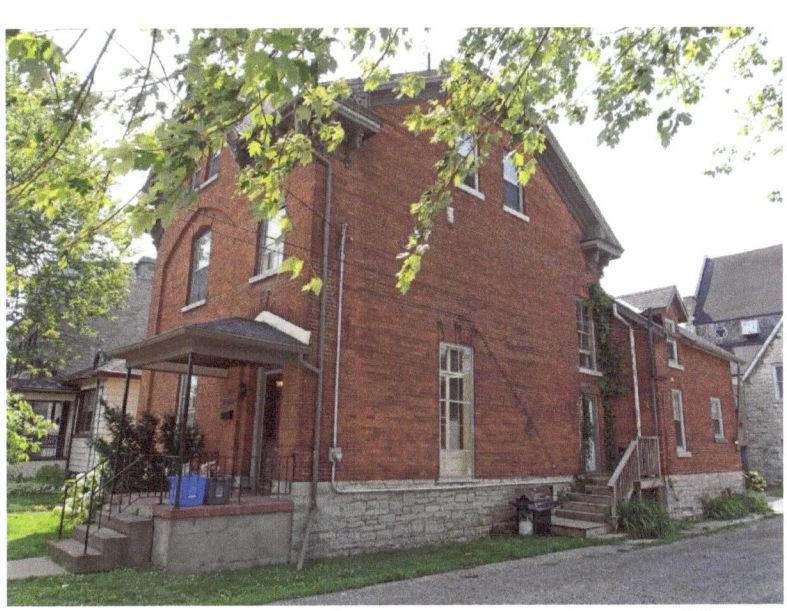

30 Colborne Street – The Rev. Harvey Servage House – 2½ storey red brick

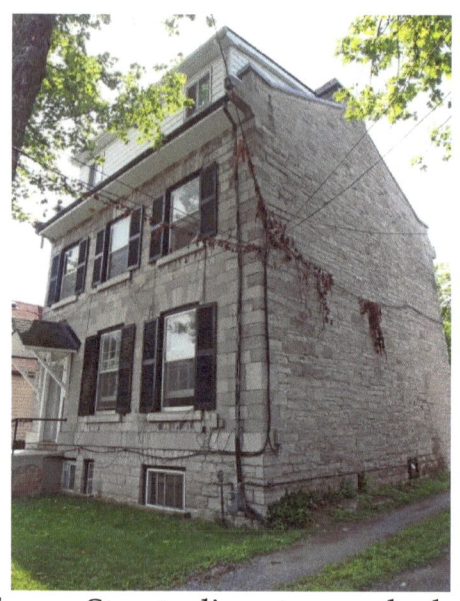

22 Colborne Street – limestone – shed dormer

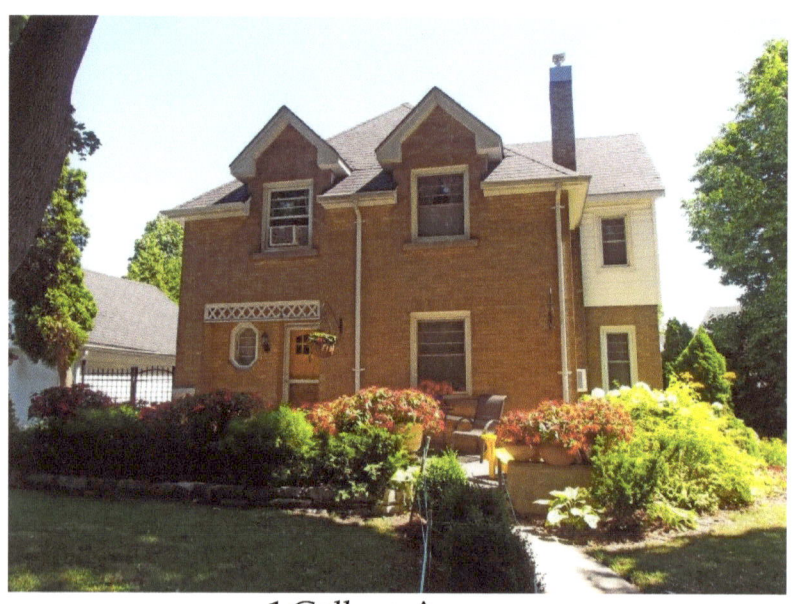

1 College Avenue

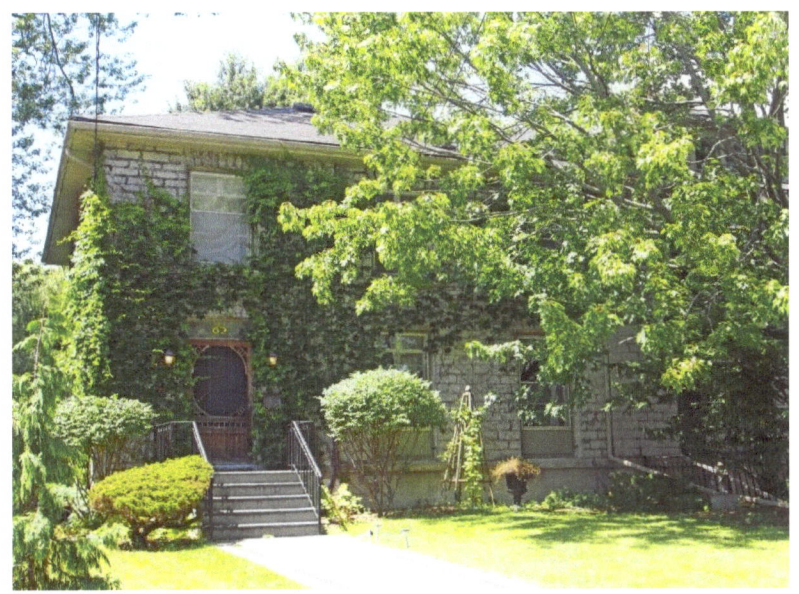

62 College Avenue – two storey limestone, hipped roof

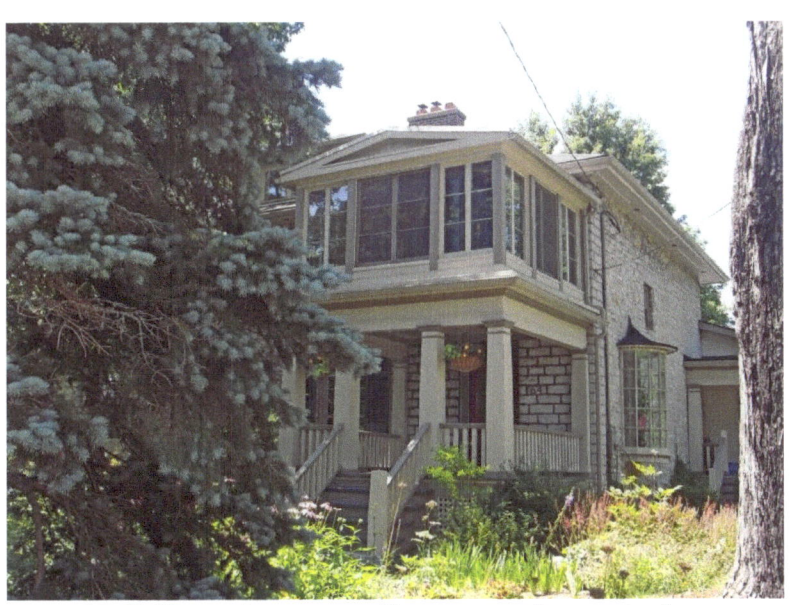

64 College Avenue – limestone, bay window

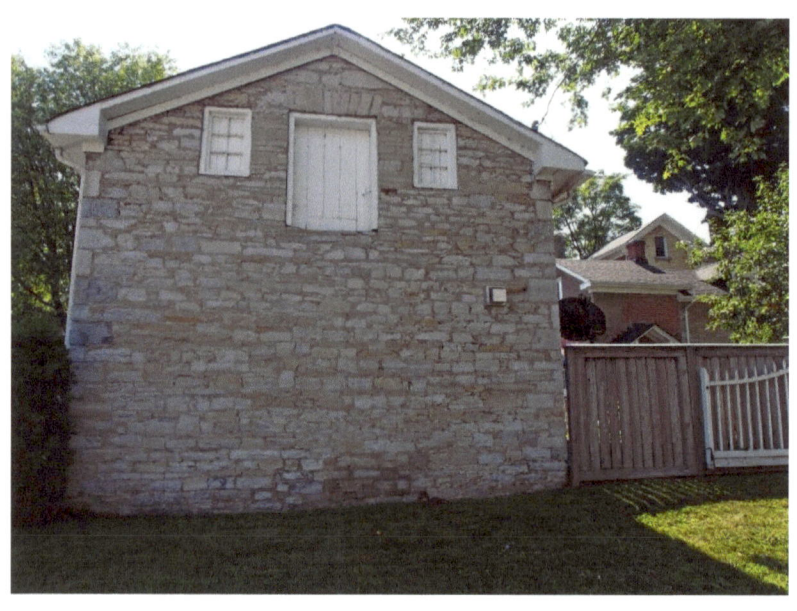

Maitland Street - limestone

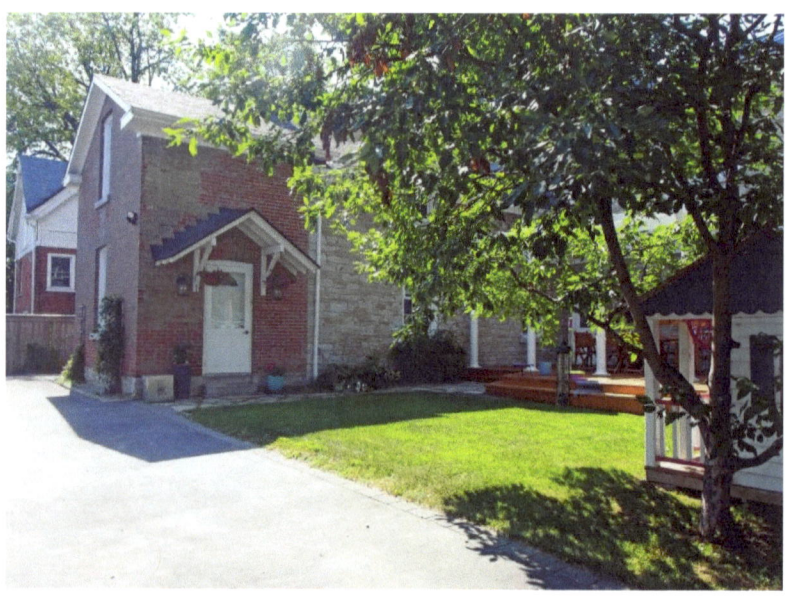

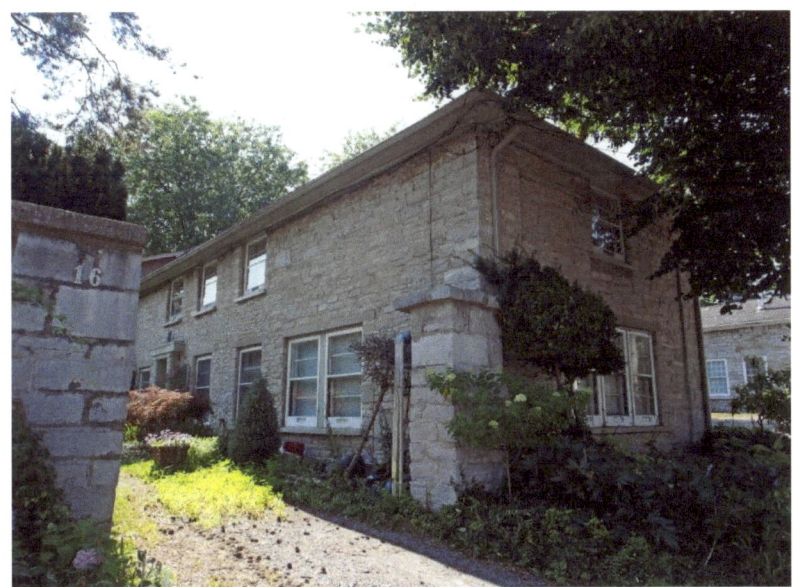

Maitland Street - limestone

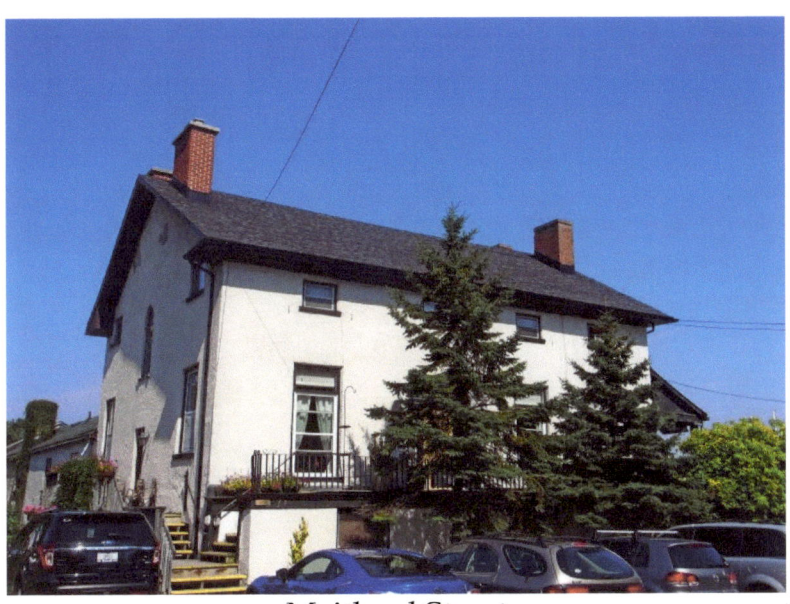

Maitland Street

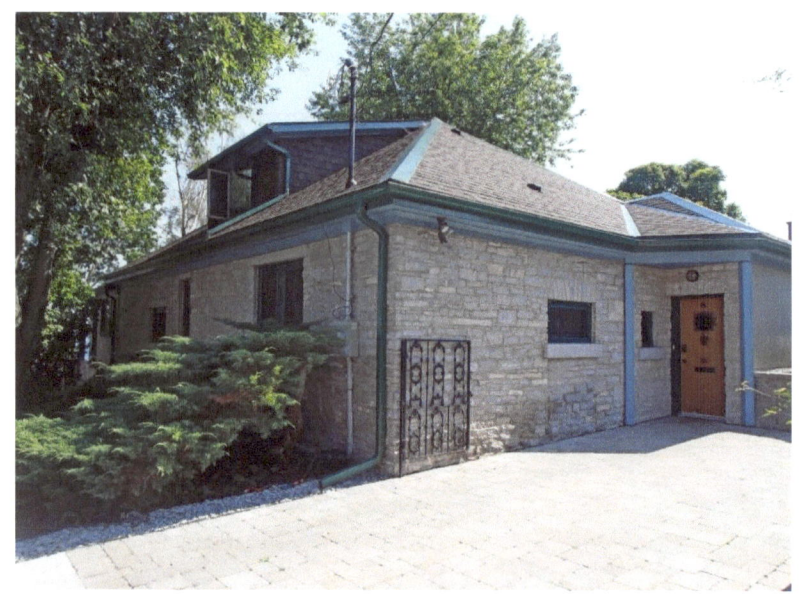

8 Maitland Street – limestone, hipped roof, dormer

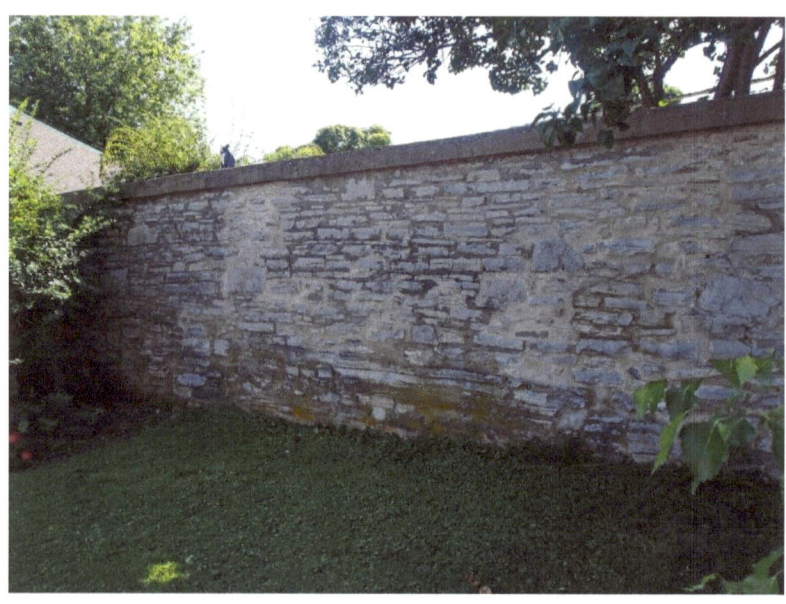

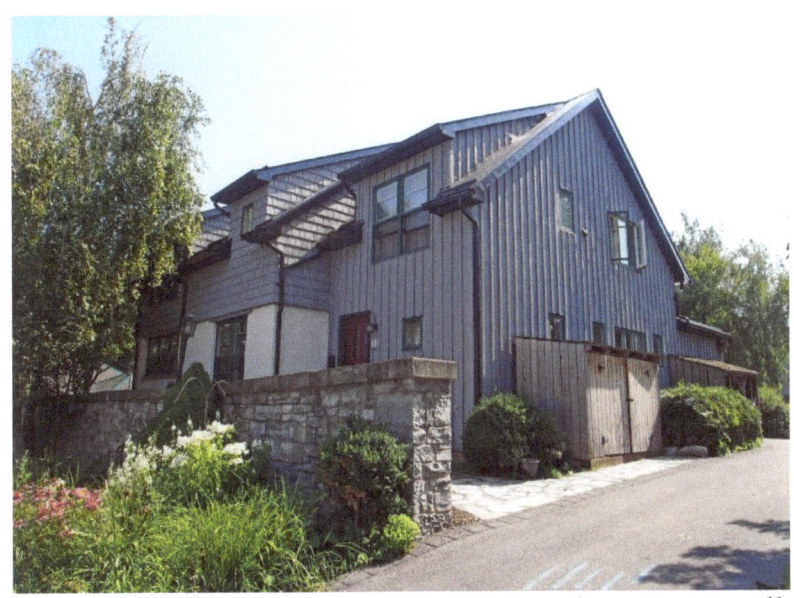

14 Maitland Street – board and batten, limestone wall

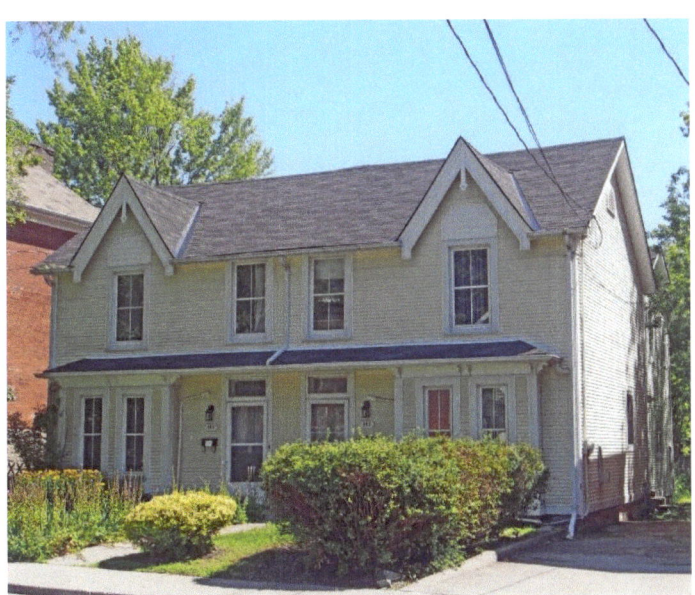

143-145 Collingwood Street – Gothic Revival – verge board trim and finial on gables

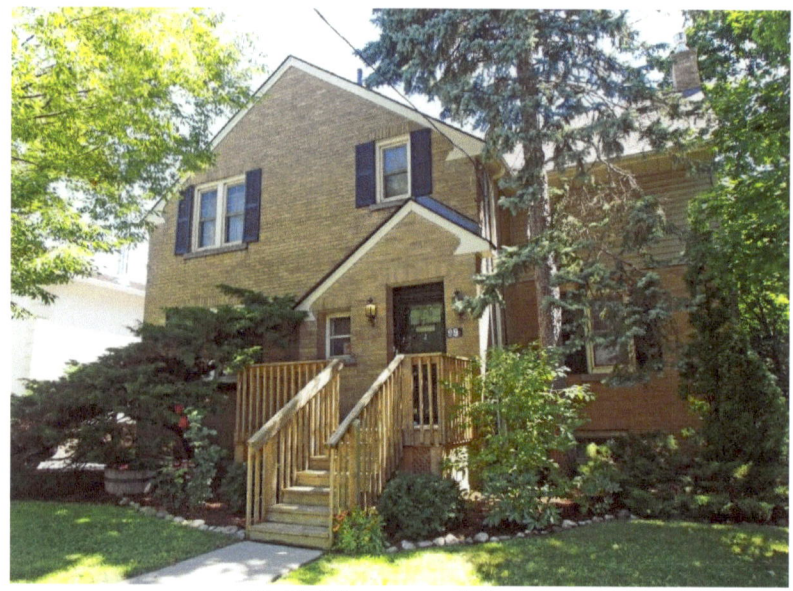

99 Collingwood Street

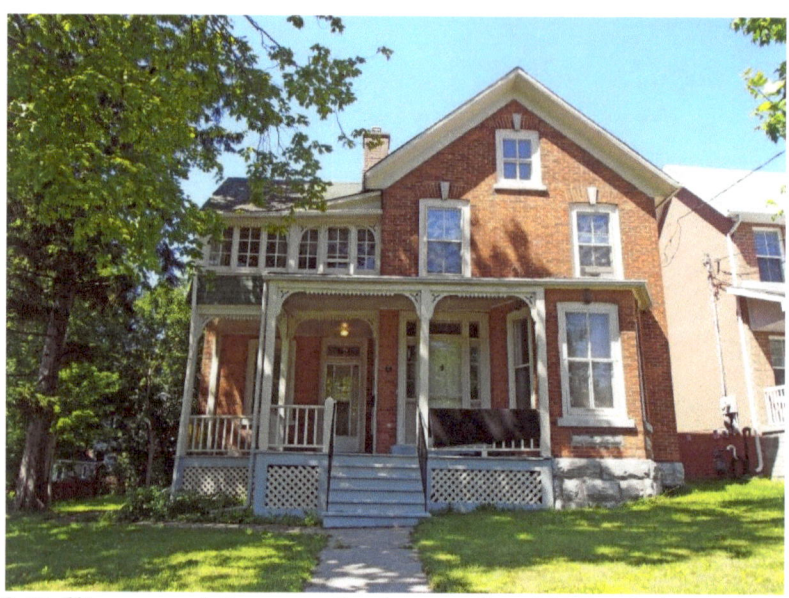

110 Collingwood Street – Inglewood c. 1888 – 2½ storey red brick, voussoirs and keystones, sidelights and transom

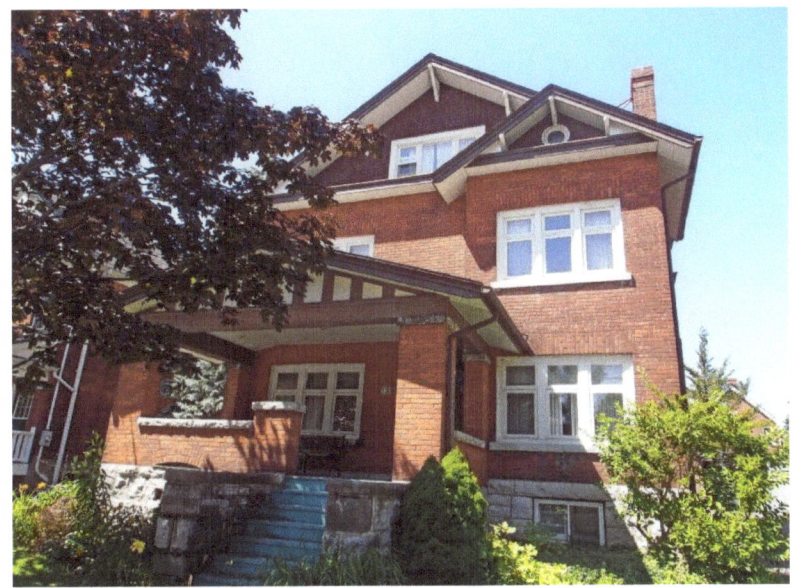

130 Collingwood Street

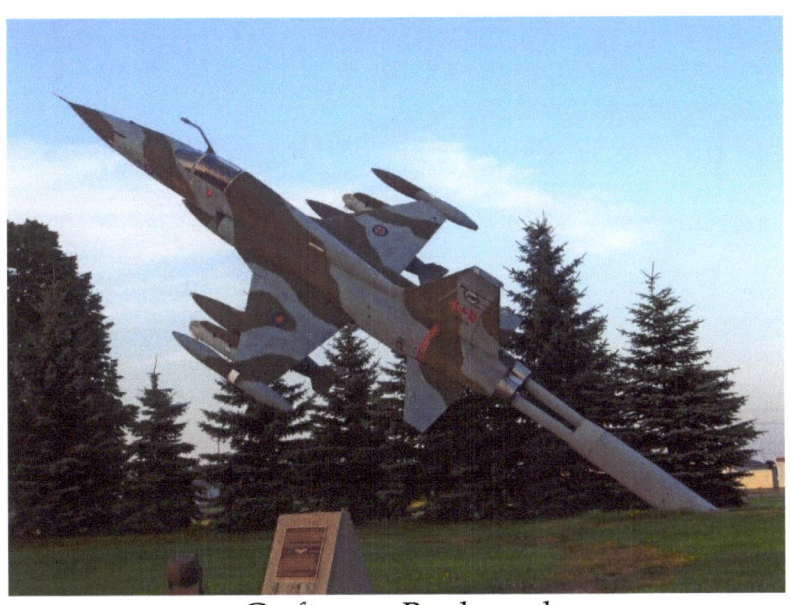

Craftsman Boulevard

The Air Force and Joint Operations

Since its very beginning, the Canadian Air Force has been supporting Joint Operations. Following distinguished service by Canadian airmen in World War I, the Canadian Air Force was formed, becoming the Royal Canadian Air Force in 1924. In the Second World War, Canadian air and ground crews played vital roles in the Battle of the Atlantic and D-Day landings affirming the importance of Air Power in Joint Operations. In the post-war years, the Canadian Air Force has continued to support the other services, seeing action in the Gulf War, in the former Yugoslavia and International Peace Support, and humanitarian operations around the world.

The Navy and Joint Operations

The Canadian Navy has a long-standing tradition of contributing to Joint Operations. During the Battle of the Atlantic, the shared efforts of the RCN and the RCAF helped keep the sea lanes open. Operations in France and Korea, as well as the Suez peacekeeping mission serve as examples of cooperation between the RCN and the Canadian Army. Today the Navy supports joint missions with a capability to defend operating areas from sea and land-based attack, as well as providing support for operations ashore.

The Army and Joint Operations

The Army provides Joint Operations with the capability to seize and hold ground, dominate terrain, and physically protect land-based resources and people. It is the Army that will ultimately close with and destroy the enemy. The 1942 Dieppe Raid and the 1944 Normandy invasion were Joint Operations involving units of the Canadian Army, Navy and Air Force. Today the Army is involved in joint missions around the world.

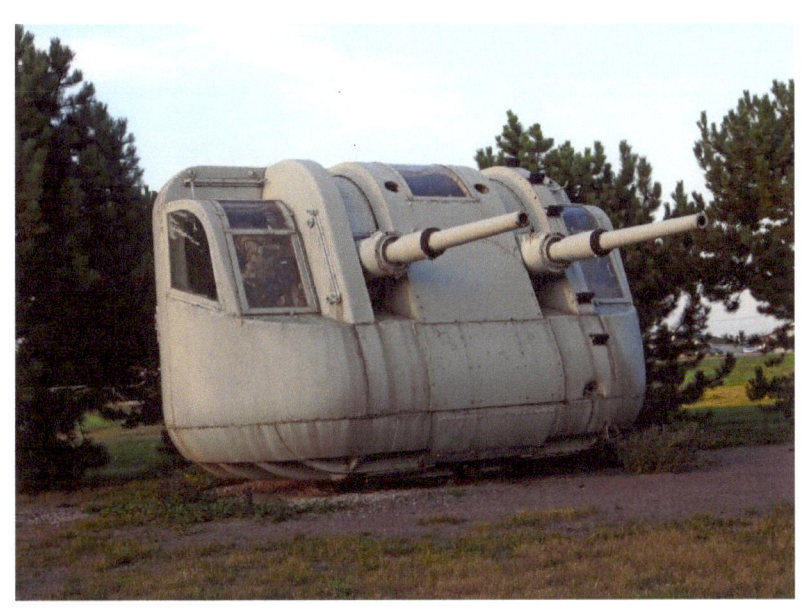

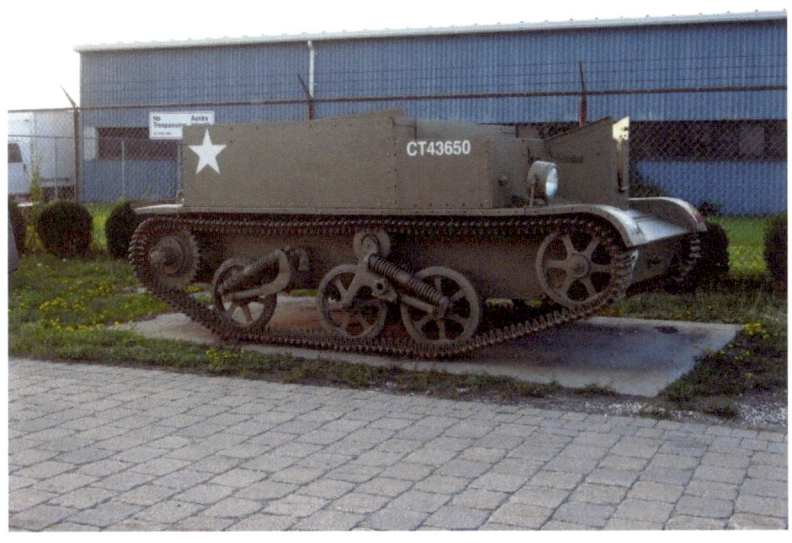

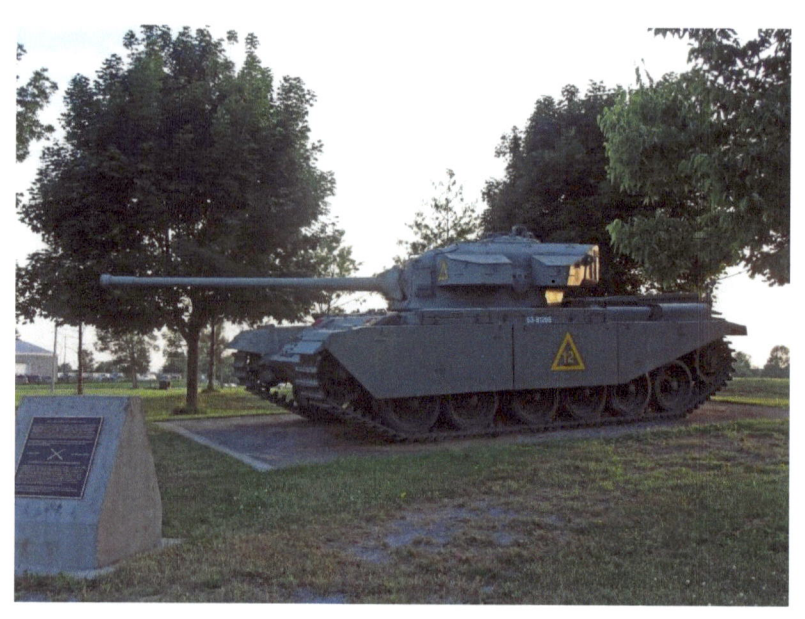

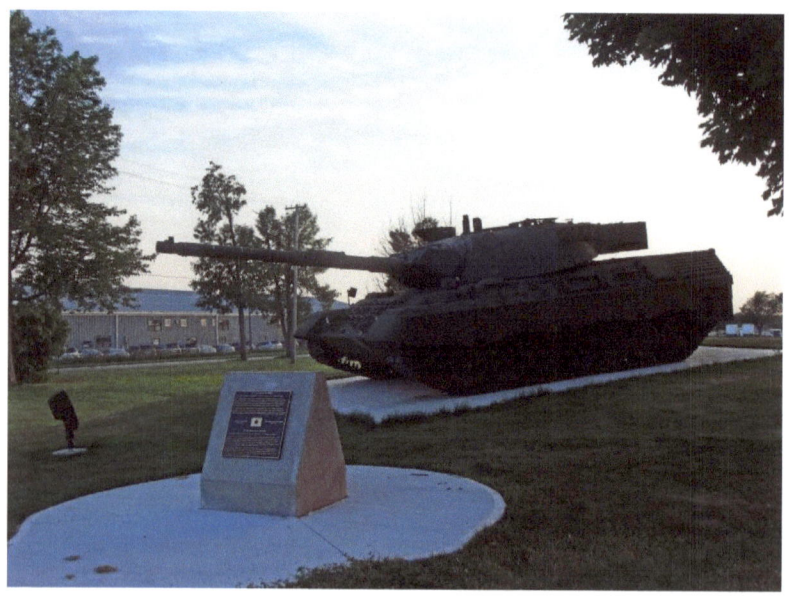

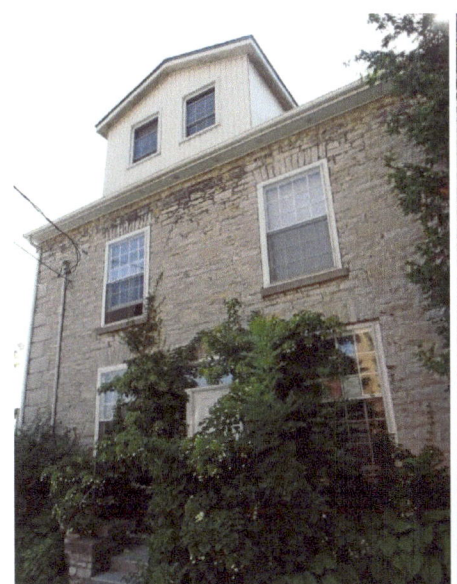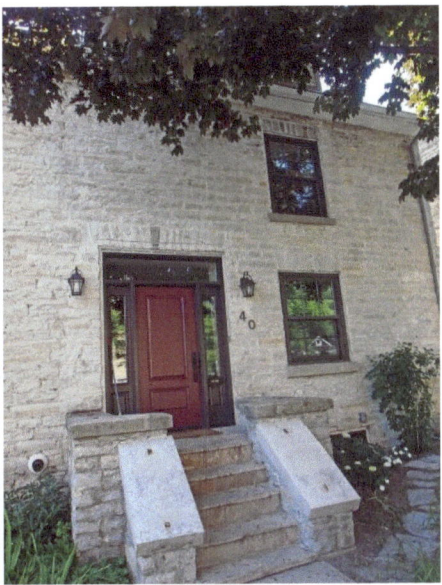

32 and 40 Simcoe Street – limestone, dormer

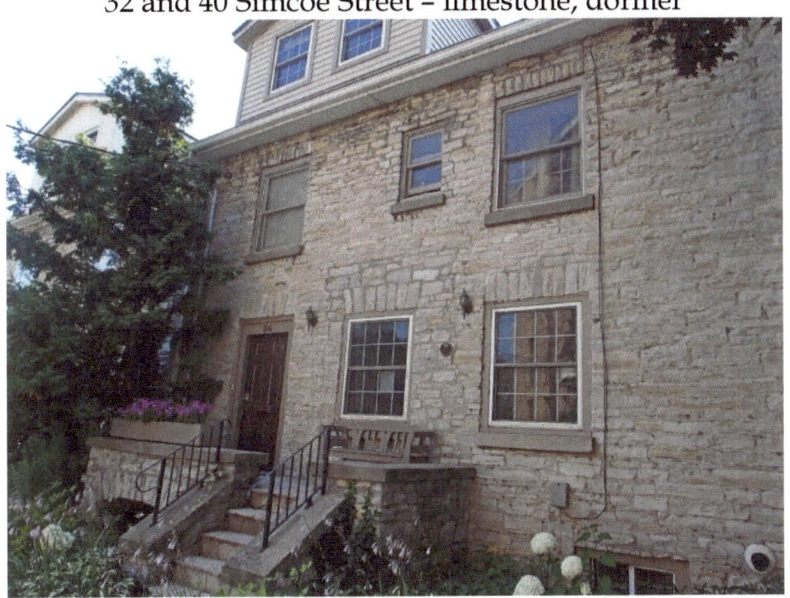

36 Simcoe Street
32, 34, and 40 Simcoe Street - built in 1842 as a triple house
John P. Bower, Tanner

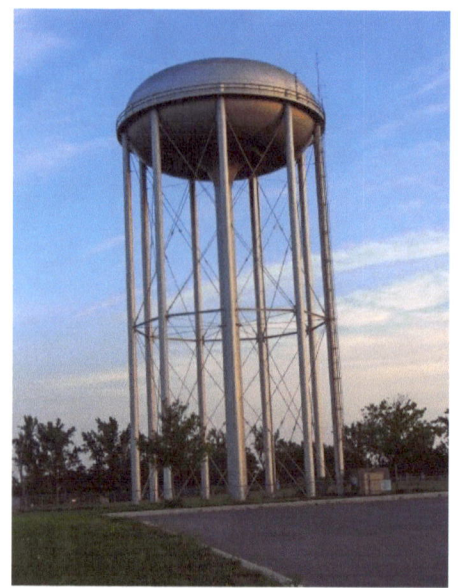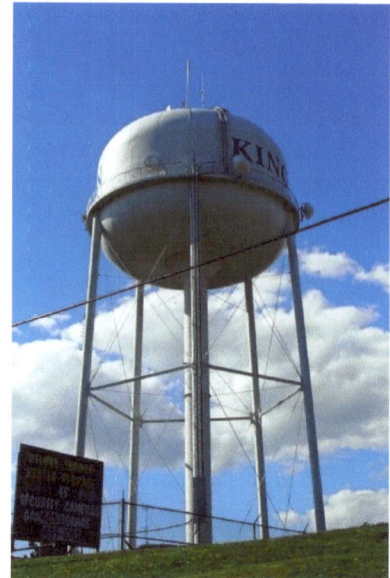

Water towers

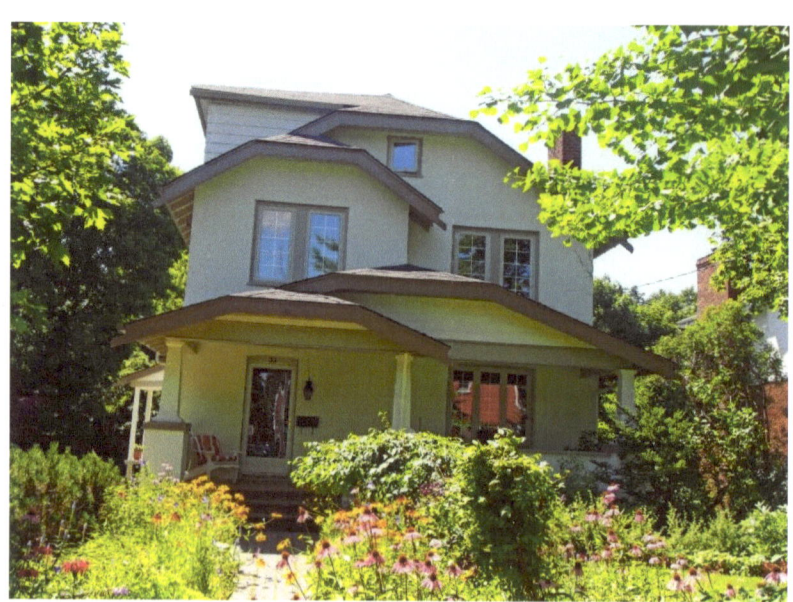

32 Edgehill Street - Vernacular

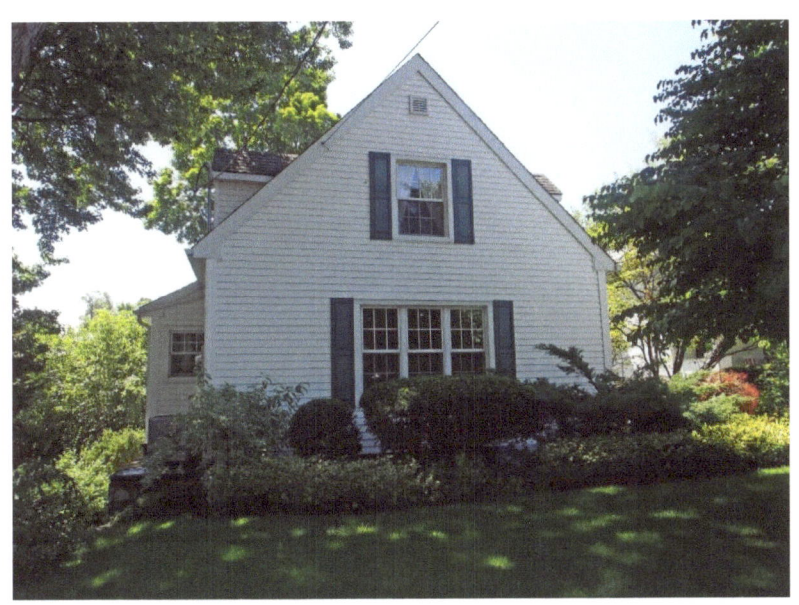

80 Edgehill Street

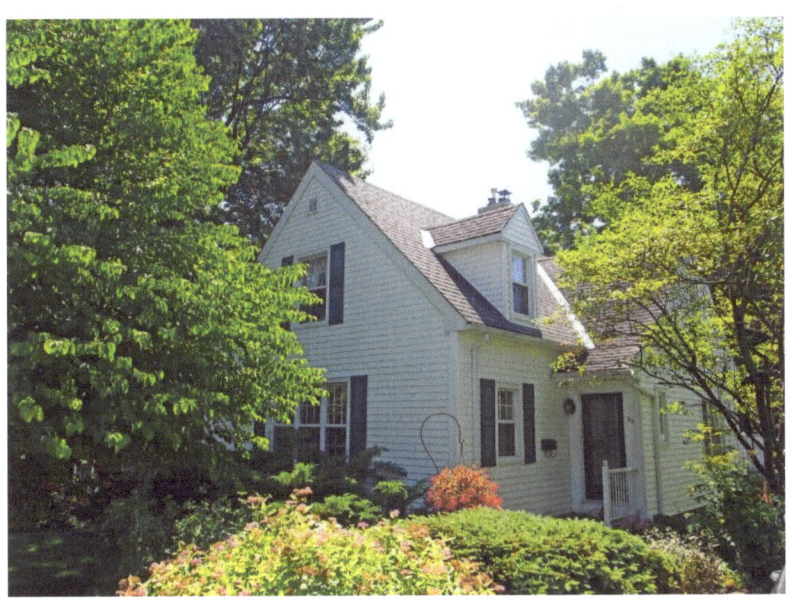

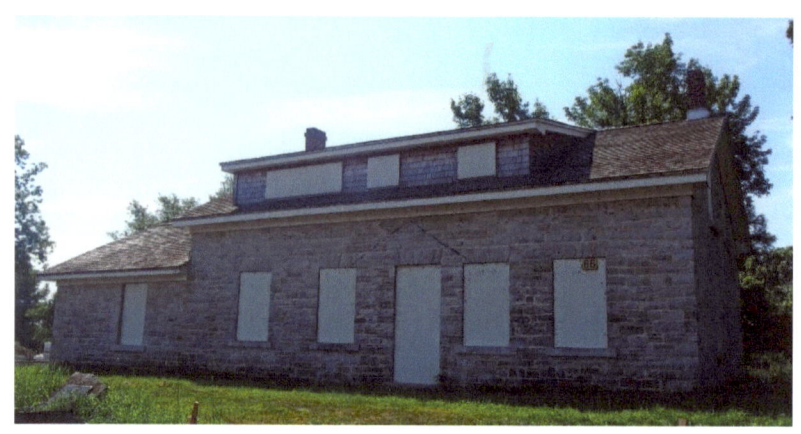

86 Sunny Acres – Peter Wartman House constructed 1803 – first stone house built on the shores of Lake Ontario between Kingston and Toronto

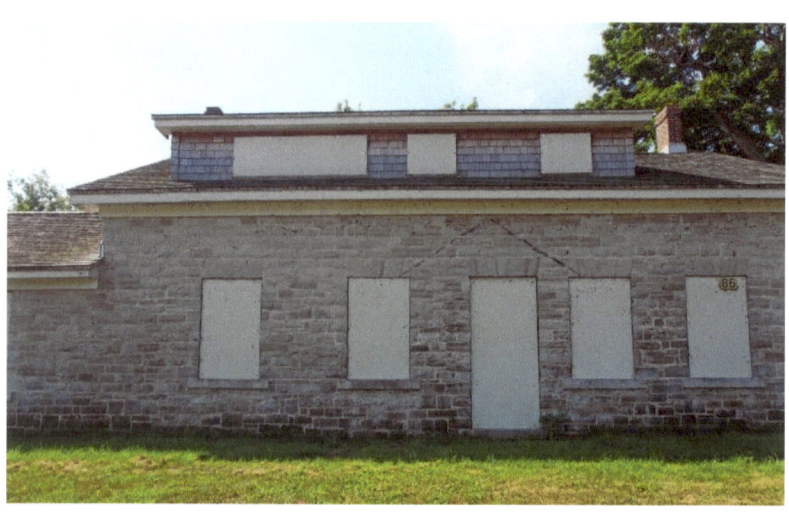

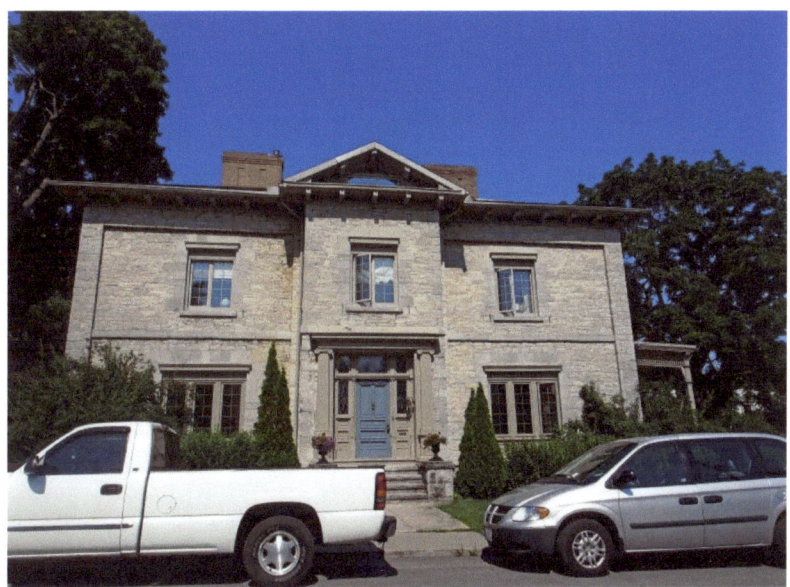

5 Emily Street – two storey limestone, frontispiece, cornice brackets, banding

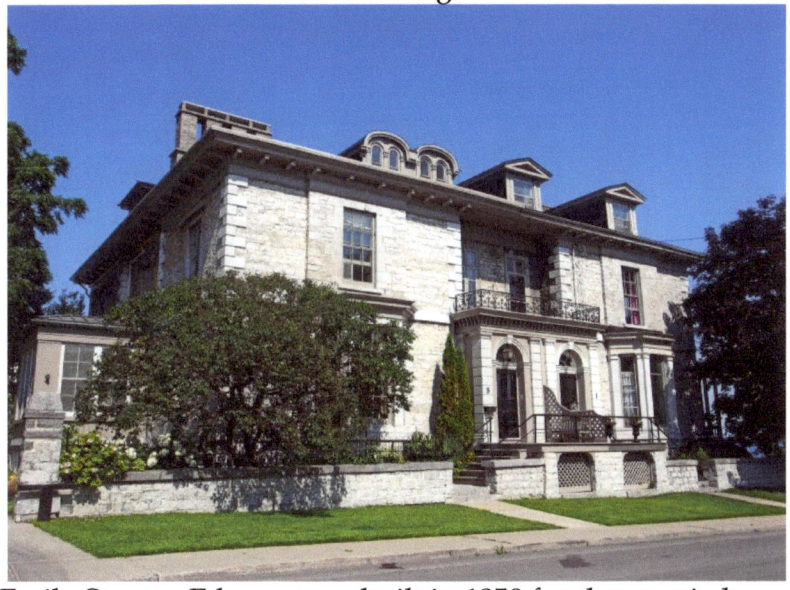

1-3 Emily Street – Edgewater – built in 1859 for the married son and daughter of John Hamilton – two round-arched doors stand together, flanked by bay windows; dormers in attic, second floor balcony, corner quoins

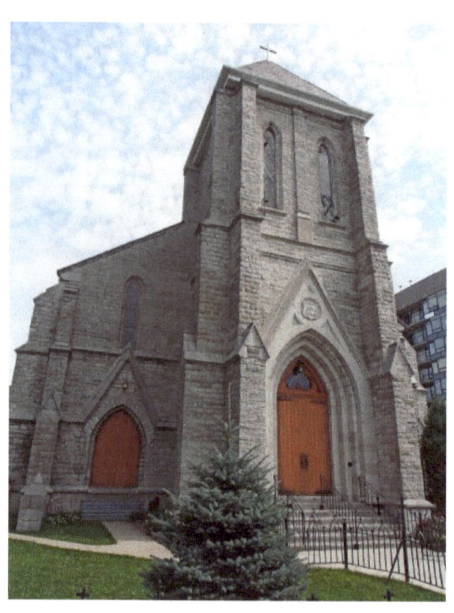

137 Queen Street – St. Paul's Anglican Church – A.D. 1845

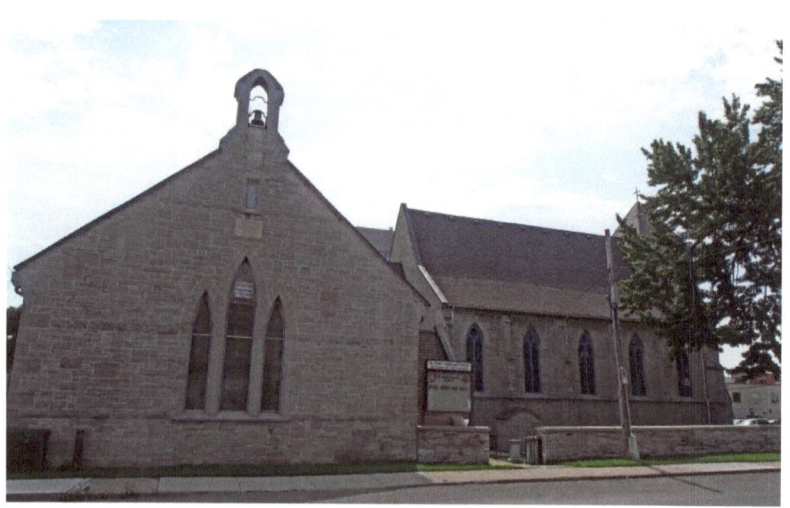

Lancet windows, buttresses

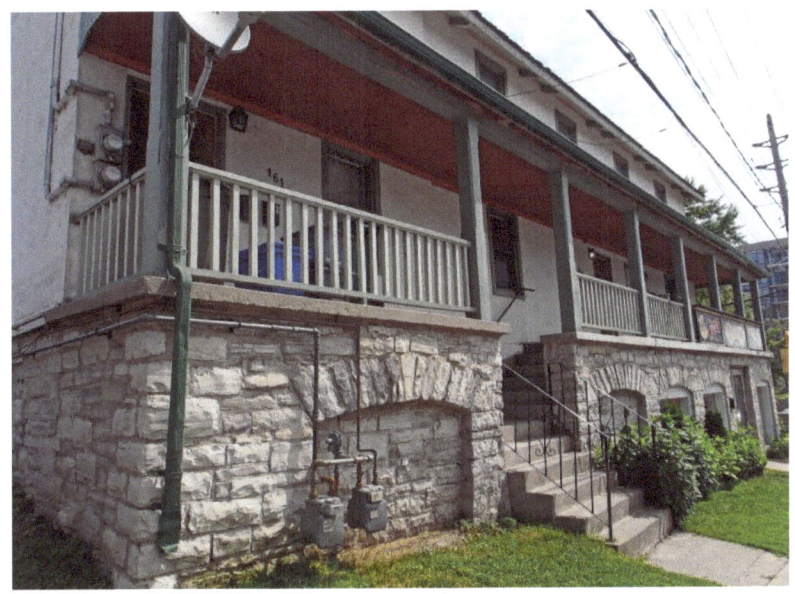

161 Queen Street

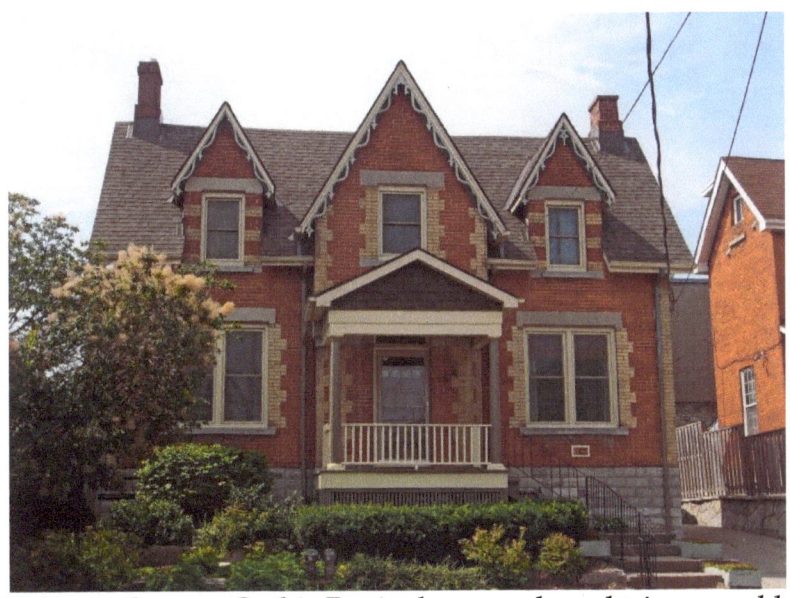

164 Queen Street – Gothic Revival – verge board trim on gables, corner quoins, and dichromatic brickwork

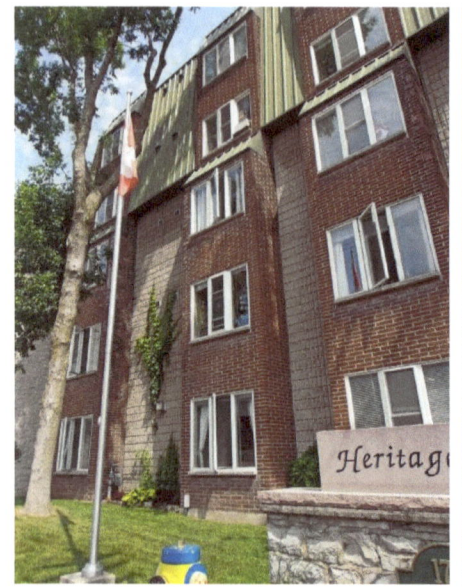

179 Queen Street

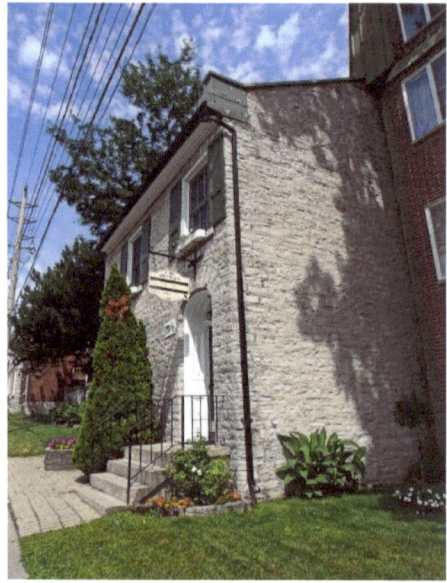

179½ Queen Street - limestone

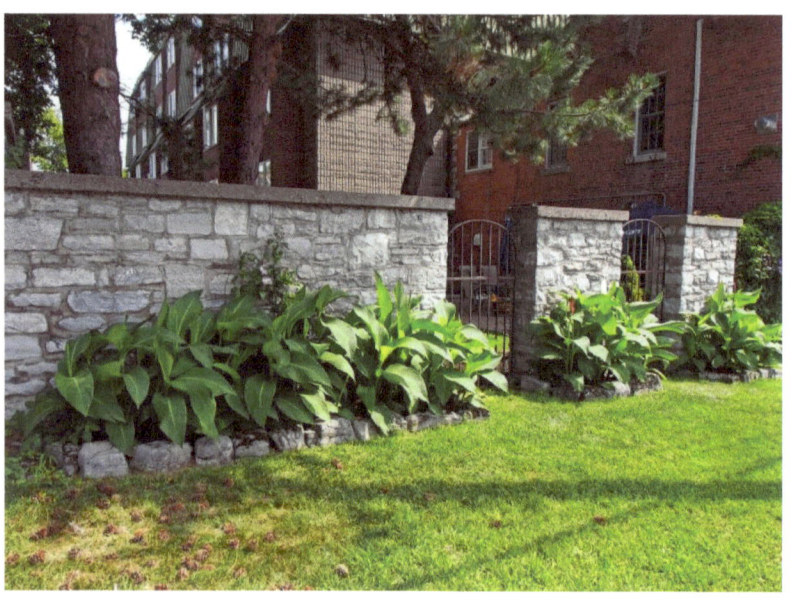

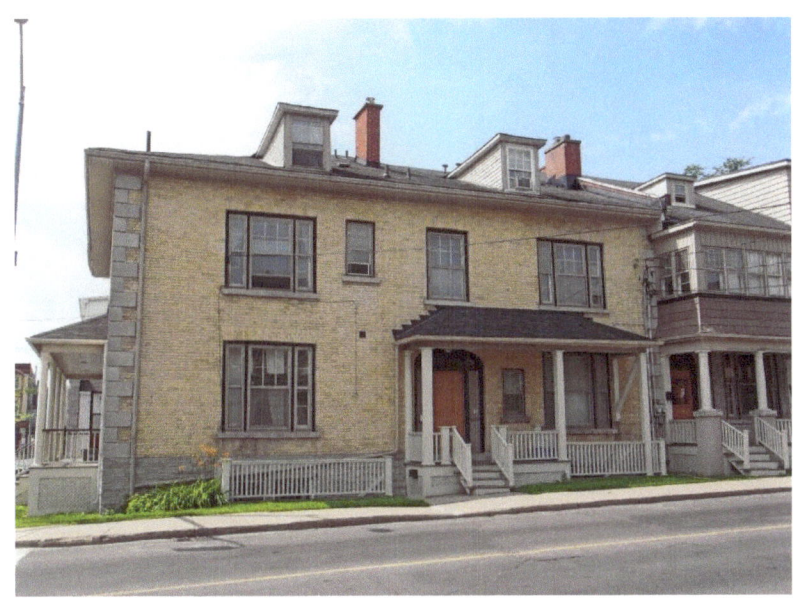

196-198 Queen Street – corner quoins, dormers

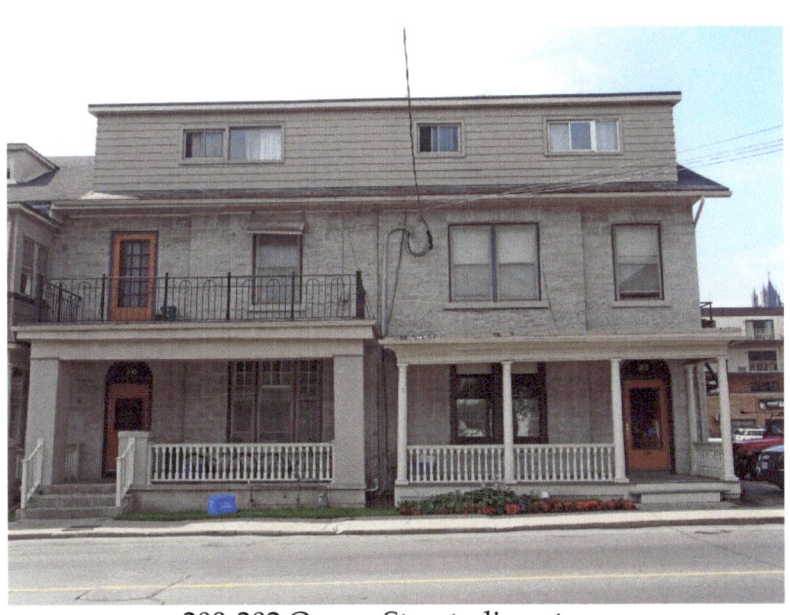

200-202 Queen Street - limestone

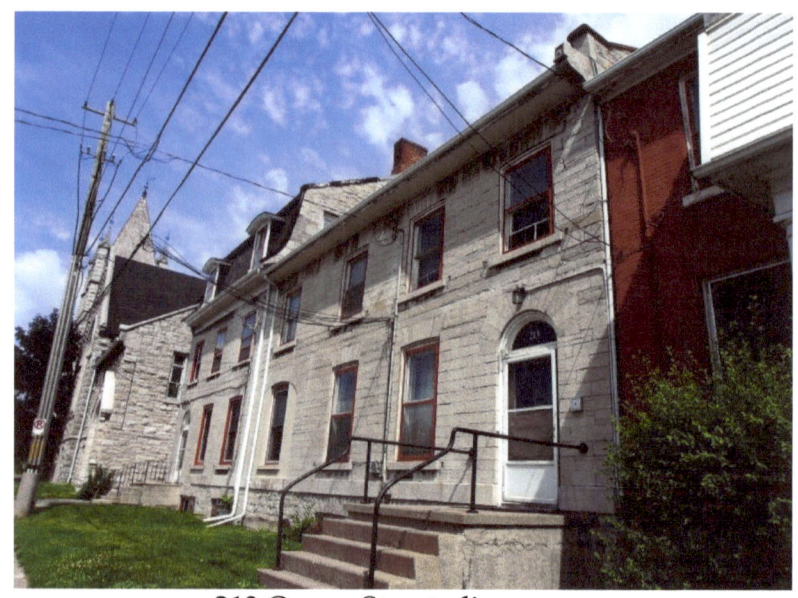

213 Queen Street - limestone

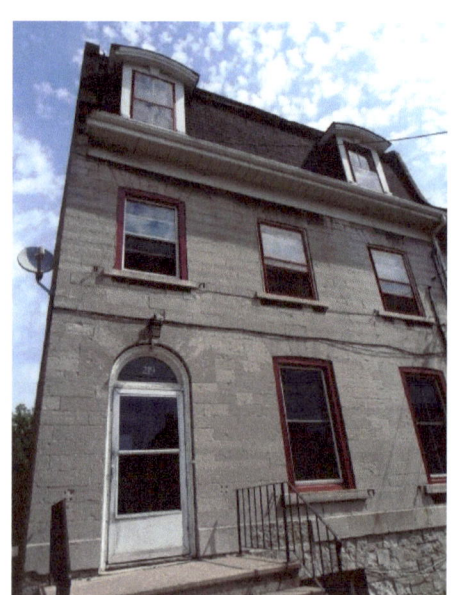

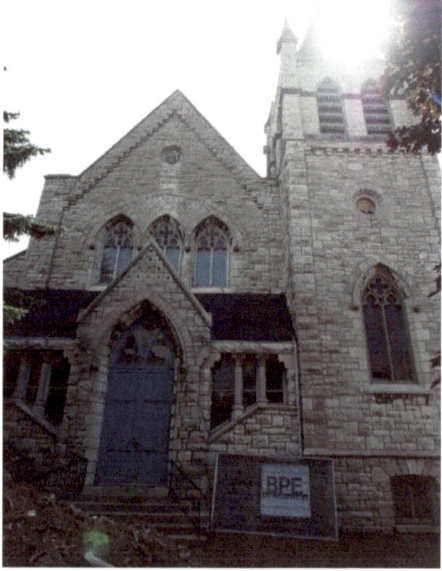

219 Queen Street
Mansard roof, dormers

limestone, Corinthian columns,
quatrefoils

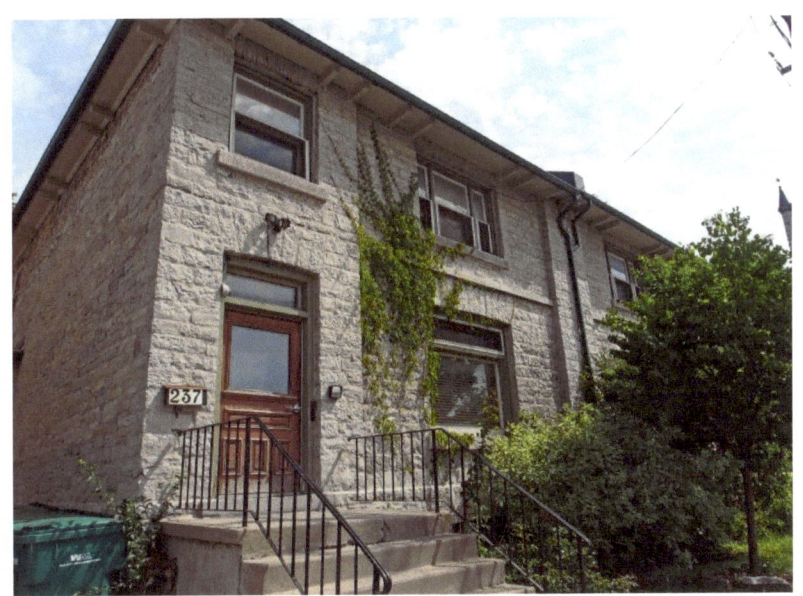

237 Queen Street

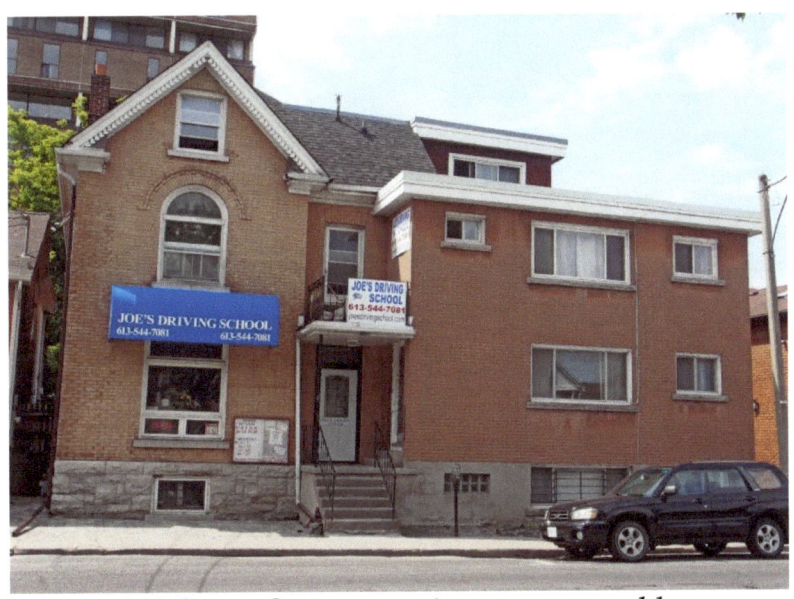

322 Queen Street – cornice return on gable

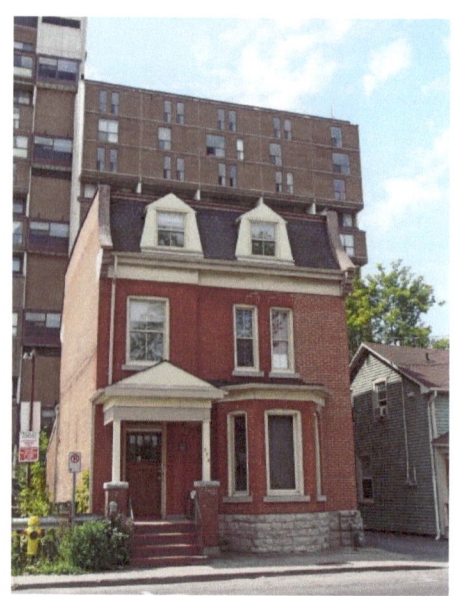

316 Queen Street

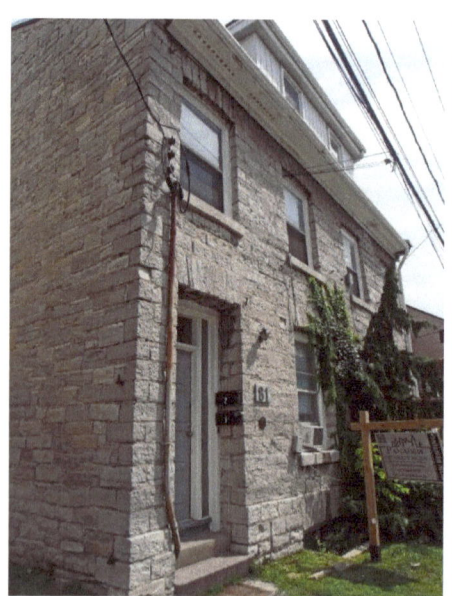

81 Queen Street

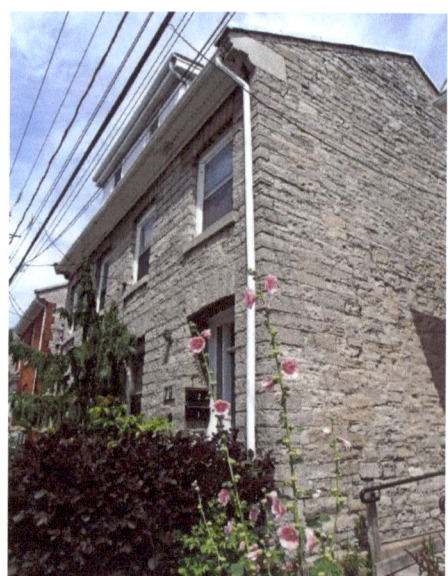

79 Queen Street

limestone

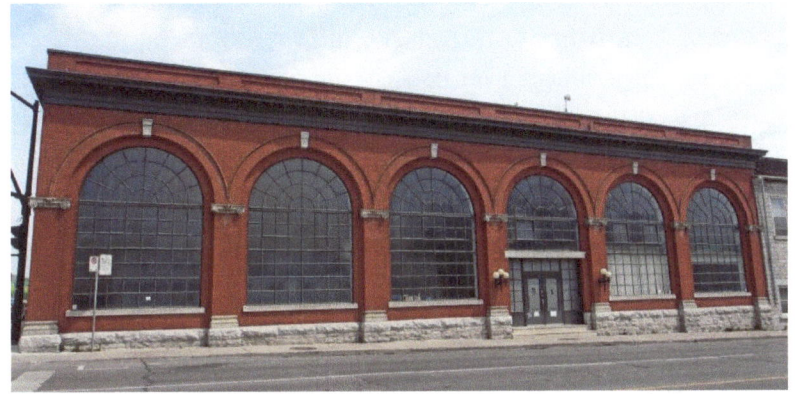

21 Queen Street – Hydro building – voussoirs with keystones

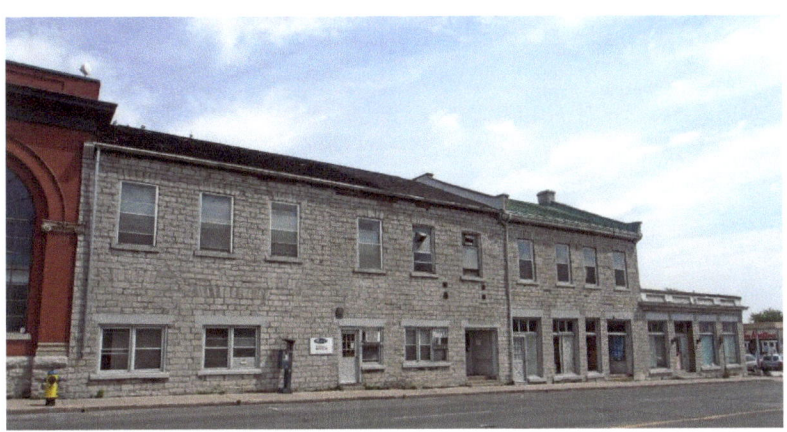

19-23 Queen Street - limestone

Architectural Terms

Balustrade: A railing system, generally around a balcony or on a second level, consisting of balusters and a top rail Example: 35 Centre Street, Page 27	
Banding: Different materials, colors or textures used in horizontal bands along a wall. Example: 180 Bagot Street, Page 12	
Bay Window: A window that projects out from a wall, in a semicircular, rectangular, or polygonal design. Used frequently in Gothic and Victorian designs. Example: 116 Bagot Street, Page 16	
Brackets: a decorative or weight-bearing structural element which forms a right angle with one side against a wall and the other under a projecting surface such as an eave or roof. Example: 116 Bagot Street, Page 16	
Buttress: a masonry structure built against or projecting from a wall which serves to support or reinforce the wall. In Canadian architecture, they are sometimes used for decoration. Example: 137 Queen Street, Page 50	

Capital: The uppermost finish or decoration on a column. A Corinthian column is characterized by a rounded capital decorated with acanthus leaves and a square abacus (the uppermost portion of a capital directly below the entablature) on tall slender columns. Example: Queen Street, Page 54	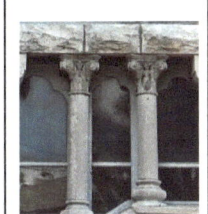
Columns were initially created to support a roof and porch structure. Originally they were free standing. Over time, builders began to build the walls between the columns so that the columns were part of the wall itself. These are called engaged columns. Engaged columns can be either structural or decorative. Example: 123 Centre Street, Page 23	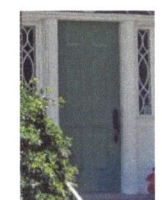
Cornice Return: decorative element on the end of a gable. Example: 322 Queen Street, Page 55	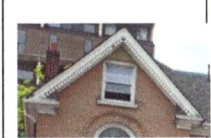
Dentil Moulding: an even series of rectangles used as ornamental decoration in cornices. Example: 116 Bagot Street, Page 16	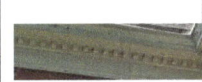
Dichromatic brickwork: the use of two colours of brick, tile or slate to decorate a façade. Example: 164 Queen Street, Page 51	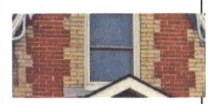
Dormer: (French for "sleep") a gable end window that pierces through the plane of a sloping roof surface to create usable space in the top floor or attic of a building by adding headroom. Example: 16 Beverley Street, Page 21	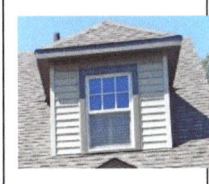

Entrance: The entrance encompasses the doorway and the inner vestibule or, in residential architecture, the covered porch. Example: 26 Centre Street, Page 28	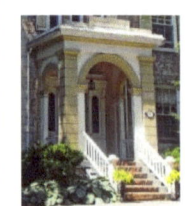
Frontispiece: a portion of the façade of a building, usually a centred doorway that is slightly raised from the rest of the building, usually has extensive ornamentation. Frontispieces are usually Classical in design with white columned porches. Example: 5 Emily Street, Page 49	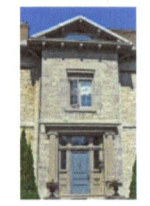
Gable: the triangular portion of a wall between the edges of a sloping roof. Example: 69-75 Colborne Street, Page 33	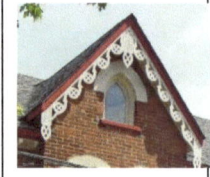
Hipped Roof: a roof where all sides slope downwards to the walls with no gables. Example: 180 Bagot Street, Page 12	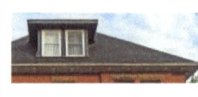
Keystones and Voussoirs: a voussoir is a wedge-shaped element used in building an arch. A keystone is the central stone that locks all the stones into position, allowing the arch to bear weight. A keystone is often enlarged and embellished. Example: 110 Collingwood Street, Page 40	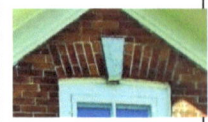

Lancet Window: a tall, narrow window with a pointed arch at its top. Example: 137 Queen Street, Page 50	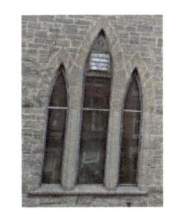
Mansard Roof: This style was popularized by Francois Mansart (1598-1666), an accomplished architect of the French Baroque period and especially fashionable during the Second French Empire (1852-1870). This roof is almost flat on the top section, with two slopes on each of its sides with the lower slope at a steeper angle than the upper and having dormer windows. Example: 116 Bagot Street, Page 16	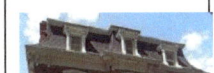
Palladian Window: a large window that is divided into three sections with the centre section larger than the two side sections and usually arched. Example: 96 Albert Street, Page 6	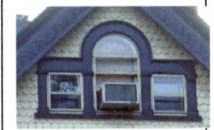
Pediment: a triangular section above the horizontal structure (entablature), typically supported by columns. The inside of the triangle is called the tympanum. Example: 96 Albert Street, Page 6	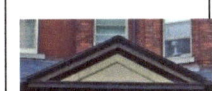
The **quatrefoil** is a type of decorative framework consisting of a symmetrical shape which forms the outline of four partially overlapping circles of the same diameter. The word quatrefoil comes from Latin and means "four leaves". Example: Queen Street, Page 54	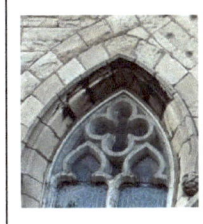

Quoin: masonry blocks at the corner of a wall, often a decorative feature, usually larger or of a different colour than the rest of the wall. Example: 196-198 Queen Street, Page 53	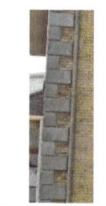
Sidelight: a window, usually with a vertical emphasis, that flanks a door, and is often used to emphasize the importance of a primary entrance. **Transom Window:** the light above the doorway, also called a fanlight. Example: 142 Albert Street, Page 7	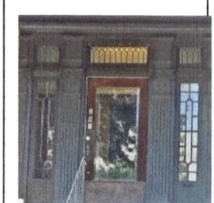
Turret: a small tower that projects from the wall of a building. Example: 144 Albert Street, Page 6	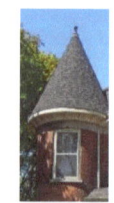
Verge board and Finial: also called bargeboards – hang from the projecting end of a roof and are often elaborately carved and ornamented. **Finial:** ornament added to the top of a gable, pinnacle, canopy or spire – a Gothic element. Example: 164 Queen Street, Page 51	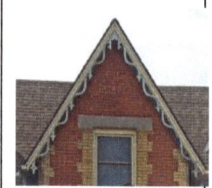
Window Hood: A **hood** is the piece found above window openings, usually of an ornate design, and covers the top third of the opening. Hoods are commonly placed above arched or curved openings on both windows and doors. Example: 116 Bagot Street, Page 16	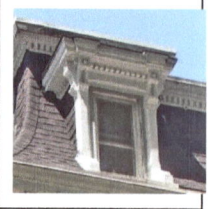

Building Styles

Edwardian, 1900-1930 – This style bridges the ornate and elaborate styles of the Victorian era and the simplified styles of the 20th century. Balanced facades, simple roof lines, dormer windows, large front porches, and smooth brick surfaces are its characteristics. Example: 208-210 Bagot Street, Page 9	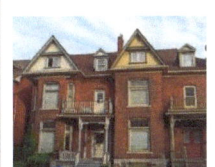
Gothic Revival, 1830-1890 – These decorative buildings have sharply-pitched gables with highly detailed verge boards, pointed-arch window openings, and dichromatic brickwork. It is a common style in Ontario. Example: 102 Centre Street, Page 23	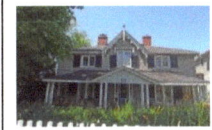
Italianate, 1850-1900 – A two story rectangular building with a mild hip roof, a projecting frontispiece, and generous eaves with ornate cornice brackets was the basis of the style; often there are large sash windows, quoins, ornate detailing on the windows, belvederes and wraparound verandahs. Italianate commercial buildings often have cast iron cresting and elegant window surrounds. Example: 138 Albert Street, Page 7	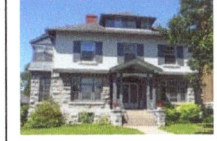

Italian Villa: This style was the first Ontario style that broke from the architectural traditions of the first settlers and imitated the harmony and balance of Classical architecture found in Northern Italian villas. The style is strictly residential and is characterized by an irregular roofline punctuated by a tall tower or campanile (bell tower). Small balconies, cantilevered eaves offering deep summer shade and arcaded porticos are standard features. Architects designing these houses were clearly after the picturesque. Example: 35 Centre Street, Page 27	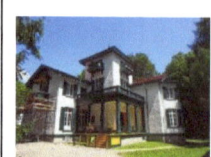
Queen Anne, 1885-1900 – This style is distinguished by an irregular outline featuring a combination of an offset tower, broad gables, projecting two-storey bays, verandahs, multi-sloped roofs, and tall, decorative chimneys. A mixture of brick and wood is common. Windows often have one large single-paned bottom sash and small panes in the upper sash. Example: 96 Albert Street, Page 6	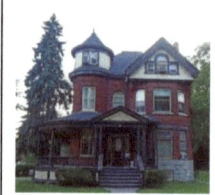
Regency Cottage, 1830-1860 – This style originated in England in 1815 and spread to Ontario later in the 19th century as British officers retired to Canada. It is a modest one-storey house with a low-pitched hip roof and has a symmetrical front façade. Example: 124 Centre Street, Page 22	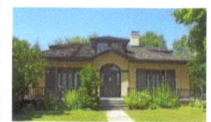

Second Empire, 1860-1880 – The mansard roof is the most noteworthy feature of this style and is evidence of the French origins. Projecting central towers and one or two-storey bays can also be present. Example: 116 Bagot Street, Page 6	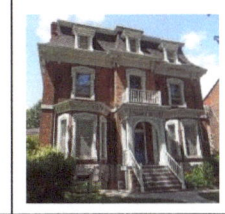
Tudor Revival – exposed timbers with stucco infill, multi-paned windows. Example: 110 Bagot Street, Page 16	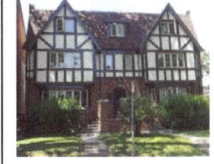
Vernacular/Traditional Mode 1638 - 1950 Influenced but not defined by a particular style, vernacular buildings are made from easily available materials and exhibit local design characteristics. Example: 108 Albert Street, Page 8	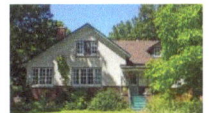